LUFTWAFFE VICTORY MARKINGS 1939–45

CASEMATE | ILLUSTRATED | SPECIAL

BALLS O' FIRE

CASEMATE | ILLUSTRATED | SPECIAL

LUFTWAFFE VICTORY MARKINGS 1939–45

PHILIPPE SAINTES

CISS0011

Published in the United States of America and Great Britain in 2021 by
CASEMATE PUBLISHERS
1950 Lawrence Road, Havertown, PA 19083, USA
and
The Old Music Hall, 106–108 Cowley Road, Oxford OX4 1JE, UK

Hardback Edition: ISBN 978-1-63624-090-9
Digital Edition: ISBN 978-1-63624-091-6

A CIP record for this book is available from the British Library

Design by Battlefield Design
Translated by Neil Page
Printed and bound by in the Czech Republic by FINIDR s.r.o.

For a complete list of Casemate titles, please contact:
CASEMATE PUBLISHERS (US)
Telephone (610) 853-9131
Fax (610) 853-9146
Email: casemate@casematepublishers.com
www.casematepublishers.com

CASEMATE PUBLISHERS (UK)
Telephone (01865) 241249
Email: casemate-uk@casematepublishers.co.uk
www.casematepublishers.co.uk

Published by arrangement with Editions Léla Presse, Le Vigen, France and based on their book: *DÉRIVES & VICTOIRES T.II: Les marques des victoires aériennes de la chasse allemande au cours de la Seconde Guerre mondiale* by Philippe Saintes

Title page image: Meister at the controls of his Bf 110.
Contents page background: The Bf 110C of Lt. Drewes undergoing maintenance at Jever, where 4./ZG 76 was stationed from September 1940 until its departure for Iraq in May 1941.
Contents page image: One of Galland's victims, a stricken Spitfire.

Contents

The rudder victory markings displayed on the Bf 109 F-4 W.Nr. 13181 "White 1" of Oblt. Heinrich Setz, commander of 4./JG 77, at Kastornoye on the Eastern Front, following the 109th claim made by Setz on August 3, 1942. The three black bars represent the 50th (March 19, 1942), 80th (June 19, 1942) and 100th (July 24, 1942) victories returned by the Staka. The Obfw. in the photo is Karl Bickelmann, the ace's armourer.

Timeline

September 1, 1939: Germany invades Poland. Two days later, Britain and France declare war on Germany.

October 1939–April 1940: The "Phoney War."

April 9, 1940: Germany invades Denmark and Norway.

May 10, 1940: Hitler launches Blitzkrieg against the Low Countries.

July 10–October 31, 1940: The "battle of Britain."

September 5, 1940: Ace von Werra shot down and taken POW in Kent.

April 6–June 1941: Germany invades the Balkans and Greece.

June 22, 1941: Operation *Barbarossa*: the invasion of the USSR.

July 3, 1941: Ace Wilhelm Balthasar KIA in France.

December 5, 1941: Ace Adolf Galland promoted to general and new Inspector of Fighters.

July 17, 1942: Ace (shipping specialist) Frank Liesendahl KIA off Brixham.

July 31, 1942: Ace Max-Hellmuth Ostermann KIA on Eastern Front.

September 6, 1942: Heinz-Arnold Stahlschmidt becomes third top N. Africa ace with kill #59.

October 23, 1942: Battle of El Alamein.

November 23, 1942: Soviet offensive traps German 6th Army in Stalingrad.

March 23, 1943: Ace Joachim Müncheberg suffers fatal crash in Tunisia.

Close-up of the tailfin markings on Bf 109 E-3 W.Nr. 1279 "Yellow 5" flown by Fw. Hans Troitzsch of 6./JG 77. The badge of 6./JG 77 was a penguin. When Winston Churchill became Prime Minister in May 1940, his initials attracted the mockery of German propaganda and were also made fun of by Luftwaffe personnel. Here, in a rare example of German word-play: the JG 77 penguin is seen doing his business in the WC. The rudder of Troitzsch's "Emil" was often photographed by war correspondents. This picture was probably taken at Aalborg in April 1940, when II./JG 77 was deployed on Operation Weserübung in Scandinavia. Troitzsch claimed one of the first RAF bombers shot down, a 9 Squadron Wellington, part of a force attempting to attack Kriegsmarine vessels off Wilhelmshaven on September 4, 1939.

May 13, 1943: Axis forces surrender in North Africa.

July 5, 1943: Operation *Citadel*—the battle of Kursk—opens.

October 8, 1943: Hans Philipp KIA after 206 kills.

March 29, 1944: Ace Hermann Graf claims his final two kills (211 & 212) near Hanover.

April 27, 1944: Ace Kurt Ubben shot down and KIA in France.

June 6, 1944: D-Day, the Allied landings in Normandy.

June 22, 1944: Operation *Bagration*, the Soviet summer offensive, opens.

August 15, 1944: Operation *Dragoon*, the Allied landings in the South of France.

December 16–27, 1944: Battle of the Bulge, Ardennes.

December 23, 1944: Ace Heinrich Bartels KIA over the Rhine.

January 1, 1945: Operation *Bodenplatte*. The Luftwaffe is eviscerated.

March 3, 1945: Night-fighter ace Martin Drewes claims his final kill (#49) over Münster.

March 7, 1945: Night-fighter ace Ludwig Meister claims his final kill (#39) over Kassel.

May 7, 1945: Unconditional surrender of German forces to Allies.

Introduction

Throughout the history of warfare, the victors have always recorded their achievements, or at least given some echo to their exploits. The irregulars of the Ottoman Army, the Bashi-bazouks, exhibited the severed ears of their victims. American Indians would tear the scalps off the defeated, while the white settlers of the Wild West carved notches in their rifle butts for each opponent killed.

The scoreboard of a German ship-mounted anti-aircraft battery.

The two World Wars were naturally no exception to the rule. To illustrate their successes, soldiers and aviators compiled and displayed "visual" records of their victories. The most interesting markings were those displayed on aircraft. They varied according to the aircraft type and the mission flown—bomber, fighter, ground support—and ranged from a simple bar to more elaborate markings, including the silhouettes of downed aircraft or bombed ships and so forth. This book aims to give a quick overview of the victory decorations and "scoreboards" painted on the rudders/tailfins of German day and night fighters, which displayed some of the most "sophisticated" sets of victory markings seen during World War II.

The gun barrel of the StuG III commanded by Knight's Cross holder Walther Oberloskamp of Sturmgeschutz-Abteilung 667, seen in May 1943 displaying an impressive number of white-painted bands, each represents a destroyed vehicle.

As a rule, Luftwaffe fighter scoreboards were at their most intricate and detailed during the early years of conquest as large numbers of aces ran up huge successes, especially in the East against largely ill-prepared and weaker opponents. Victory markings applied to night fighters (*Nachtjagd*) were often even more detailed than those of the day fighters (*Tagjagd*), possibly as a result of the dark and subdued camouflage finish on these types of aircraft. The placement of the victory listings varied over time. Initially—and taking as their cue the recordkeeping of the aces of the Condor Legion in Spain—the bars were painted logically on the tailplane of the fighter, under the swastika. However, the swastika made it difficult to keep an accurate tally as the lack of space tended to limit the number of bars. Moreover, it was soon discovered that, in the event of accident or damage incurred in combat, it was much more practical to paint victory bars on the rudder, which very often remained intact, and which could also be easily dismantled and refitted on any replacement or new aircraft.

Silhouettes of tanks painted on the tail of an Hs 129 ground support aircraft in the USSR, the "scorecard" of its pilot.

The bombs painted on this 381st BS/310th BG B-25 "Balls of fire" display the number of missions flown by its crew.

The crew of this Do 17 have claimed the destruction of a number of balloons, along with what appear to be three aerial victories.

The swastikas painted under the cockpit of this P-51 illustrate this pilot's record of victories.

This Ju 88 of KG 30 in the Mediterranean has apparently sunk a number of vessels …

… as has this KG 40 Fw 200. Note that the large swastika on the Ju 88's tailfin has rendered it a little difficult for the ground crew to keep the "scoreboard" updated. The tall vertical tail of the "Condor" was more suitable for neat work.

During the early months of the war, some of the victory markings applied were quite sophisticated. Many victory bars (cf. Machold, Galland, or Bertram) indicated the date and place of the *Luftsieg*, or aerial victory. Others displayed Belgian, French, or British roundels to specify the nationality of the victim. During the battles over England, probably due to the difficulties in pinpointing the exact location of a downed enemy aircraft, this practice seems to have declined although many pilots (but also mechanics) continued to top a painted-on victory "bar" with a symbol to identify the nationality of the victim. However, given the enormous number of "holed" or torn aircraft tailfins and rudders requiring repair and "patches" following combat, the often-overworked ground crews and mechanics were often content to paint simple bars to "publicize" the exploits of their pilots. This simplification (or increasing "standardization") explains the difficulties in identifying many rudder photographs as early as 1942.

But a victory must always be claimed. Contrary to the Italian fighter arm (for example), the Luftwaffe encouraged emulation and sought to stimulate competition and healthy rivalry by attributing each *Luftsieg* to an individual pilot. The notion of "shared" victories did not exist. This was not normally a problem if the wreckage came down in friendly territory. When combat took place over enemy lines or over the sea, it was necessary to rely on the eyewitness testimony of other pilots (including the wingman) and sometimes even of the crew of the downed plane, if captured.

A mechanic paints a third victory bar on the fin of a Bf 109E. Although this photo was taken on December 18, 1939, during the famous "German Bay Massacre," no German fighter engaged in this battle had achieved this score (several had two victories to their credit). In many instances victory bars were marked up soon after combat and prior to any "official" verification. Of course, this photo may have been produced by the propaganda services—this was of course another "role" which the rudder or victory scoreboard fulfilled.

The crew of this ZG 76 Bf 110 have indicated the nationality of their opponents by painting the flags of Belgium, France, the Netherlands, the Scandinavian countries, and Great Britain under the cockpit sill of their machine. Even early on in the war this heavy fighter unit crew have enjoyed a "well-filled" career.

However, this scenario only applied to combat between small groups of planes. During clashes between large numbers of fighters, the same machine could likely take a burst of fire from any number of attackers—each in good faith going on to file a claim for a victory. Another source of confusion arose with the appearance of Allied heavy bomber formations in 1942. It was self-evident that a pilot who had damaged a "Flying Fortress" (or *Viermot*, a four-engined aircraft) and then forced it out of its "defensive box" or "*Pulk*," had made the aircraft more vulnerable and at risk of further attack. A system of points was set up to reflect this particular achievement, with one point for this "*Herrauschuss*" (HSS or "shooting out") and two points being then allocated to the pilot who delivered the coup de grâce. Of course, on occasion, misunderstandings led to duplicate claims and the very likely refusal to allocate and confirm a victory credit that may have already been painted up on an aircraft rudder. It can therefore be somewhat difficult to follow a particular pilot's score. It remains the case that this is the sort of information that can be "deciphered" on the rudders of the German aces when one knows how to "read" them.

This book includes both day fighter aces (*Tagjagd*) and night fighter aces (*Nachtjagd*). The aces are broadly listed according to their main area of operations in World War II. There is an element of overlap as several aces served on more than one front. In this case, the ace is listed in the area where he scored the bulk of his victories. Their victory lists are reproduced in full as they indicate over time the appearance in the skies of new adversaries—British, French, Yugoslav, Soviet, American—and the different types of aircraft encountered (e.g. Hurricane, Morane, Spitfire, P-51). As far as possible an attempt has been made to identify the unit of the opponent, particularly for those victories claimed in the West.

Calais-Marck, March 1941. In the mess, the 2./LG 2 victory board is kept up to date.

Barbarossa, June 1941. At the start of the campaign in the East, an unidentified pilot paints a victory bar on his machine. The red star of course identifies the victim as a Soviet aircraft.

1

Day Fighter Aces: East

In this chapter we look at the careers of eight Luftwaffe day fighter aces who achieved, in several cases, their mammoth victory tallies on what is broadly defined as the Eastern Front. Some 45,000 Soviet aircraft were shot down during the course of the war; overall, on all fronts, 103 German pilots achieved personal victory tallies of over 100 enemy aircraft, amounting to some 15,400 planes.

We study five pilots who achieved victories of over 100: Kurt Ubben scored 111 victories, mainly on the Eastern Front but with several in the North African theater. Max-Hellmuth Ostermann achieved 102 kills, all on the Eastern Front. Herman Graf topped 200 (211) in the Rostov, Sevastopol, Stalingrad, Kharkov, and Kerch Peninsula areas. Hans Philipp, with 206 victories, just behind Graf, claimed some victories in the West, but the bulk in the Demyansk, Leningrad, Shlisselburg, and Poutilovo sectors, and Franz-Josef Beerenbrock (112) registered his victories on the Kalinin Front, and the Rjev, Viazma, and Mamonovo sectors. Two pilots in his chapter achieved scores of between 50 and 99: Walther Ohlrogge (77) and Gerhard Köppen (85) in the Kiev, Rostov, Kharkov, and Belgorod areas. We will also study Johannes Gentzen (9 kills) who claimed his victories in the opening campaign of the war during the invasion of Poland, thus becoming one of the earliest aces.

Major Johannes Gentzen

Little is known about Johannes Gentzen, who was born on April 4, 1903, in Neubrandenburg. Having initially joined the navy, he later became a pilot with the civilian company HAPAG. His first military flights were at the secret Soviet base in Lipetsk in 1932 and he joined the Luftwaffe at its inception. In April 1936, he was in charge

Bf 109s of I./ZG 2 at Gross-Stein in late August 1939, shortly before the Polish campaign. Most of the aircraft are Bf 109D-1s, but "Yellow 11" on the right is a Bf 109C-3 equipped with 20mm guns in the wings.

The Bf 109D-1 flown by the *Kommandeur* of I./ZG 2 photographed on September 10, 1939, a week after his first two victories.

of 1. Staffel of I./JG 232 when this *Gruppe* was established, flying the He 51 at Bernburg. Two years later, he commanded the unit, which was redesignated I./JG 137 on July 1, 1938, and then I./JG 231 on November 1. On May 1, 1939, the *Gruppe* was renamed I./ZG 2 and although it was conceived as a *Zerstörer* (twin-engined heavy fighter) formation, it still flew Bf 109C/Ds like the other ZGs of the time.

Hptm. Gentzen at the controls of his Bf 109D-1 "double chevron" on his return from Poland. His chief mechanic Uffz. Lösche is standing on the wing. Temporarily renamed JGr. 102, the unit adopted the "Bernburg Fighter" as its official insignia, in honor of Jagdgruppe 102's hometown. The unit was founded as I./JG 232 on April 1, 1936, in Bernburg. The badge of the *Gruppe* was retained on the Bf 110s of I./ZG 2.

Hptm. Johannes Gentzen is flanked, on the left, by Oblt. Josef Kellner-Steinmetz (Staka 3./ZG 2) and, on the right, by Oblt. Waldemar von Roon (Staka 1./ZG 2). Both *Staffelkapitäne* were killed in combat with French H-75s on November 6, 1939, while the *Kommandeur* was killed on May 26, 1940.

On August 6, 1939, I./ZG 2 moved to Gross-Stein in Silesia to prepare to take part in the Polish campaign. On September 1, 1939, under the leadership of its *Kommandeur*, this unit operated in support of the H.Gr. Süd (Army Group South) in various roles: Ju 87 escort, ground strafing, etc. Despite his advanced age for a fighter pilot, the almost-40-year-old Gentzen was to be credited with seven victories from 2 to 14 September at the controls of a "Dora," thus becoming the most talented fighter pilot (and the only ace) of the Polish campaign. Propaganda could not let the opportunity pass and did not fail to elevate Hptm. Gentzen into the limelight, his name being regularly mentioned in the publications of the time.

On September 17, I./ZG 2 returned to Germany after having pushed on to Krakow. On the 22nd of that month, the *Gruppe* moved to Lachen-Speyerdorf in anticipation of an imminent confrontation with the Western Allies on the Westwall. But the Allied forces kept a low profile and the only combat during this period only took place in the air. Probably for the

Lachen-Speyerdorf, October 1939. Close-up of the Bf 109D-1 W.Nr. 2621, decorated with seven victory bars achieved by Gentzen.

purposes of deception, I./ZG 2 was then renamed JGr 102.

Initially, the Luftwaffe was content to repel enemy intrusions from German skies. But with the mass return to the West of the units engaged in Poland, the German fighters and reconnaissance aircraft would increasingly venture over France. Gentzen's star faded somewhat on November 6, 1939, as a result of the famous "nine versus twenty-seven" confrontation between J.Gr. 102 and the Curtiss H-75 fighters of GC II/5 near Metz. In this battle, J.Gr. 102 did not claim a single victory but lost no fewer than five aircraft while suffering two fatalities and one prisoner, the fatalities being two of the *Staffelkapitäne*, Oblt. Waldemar von Roon (1./102) and Josef Kellner-Steinmetz (3./102). Although he was credited two days later with a Morane 406 near Edenkoben, Gentzen was called to Berlin to be reprimanded. But it became clear during this disastrous battle for German arms that the now obsolete Bf 109Ds had to be replaced as soon as possible by the latest "Emils." On November 12, J.Gr. 102 was withdrawn from the front.

On January 30, 1940, the *Gruppe* reverted to its I./ZG 2 designation and received Bf 110Cs, which the pilots were to convert to as quickly as possible (while crewing with a radio gunner) in preparation for the coming campaign.

On April 7, Gentzen won a ninth and final victory, partially avenging the battle of November 6 by shooting down a Curtiss of GC I/5 near Beaumont-en-Argonne.

On May 10, 1940, Major Gentzen's I./ZG 2 was at Darmstadt-Griesheim but soon moved into conquered territory to follow the advance of the front line. On May 26, 1940, it was based at an airfield in Neufchâteau, Belgium. Blenheims appeared over the *Feldflugplatz* and Gentzen raced to his aircraft with his *Gruppenadjutant*, Oblt. Hartwig Domeier. He took off in a mad dash, but the improvised runway was surrounded by trees. The rear of the Bf 110 clipped the tops of one of them and the twin-engine machine crashed. The low altitude gave the two occupants no chance and they were killed instantly.

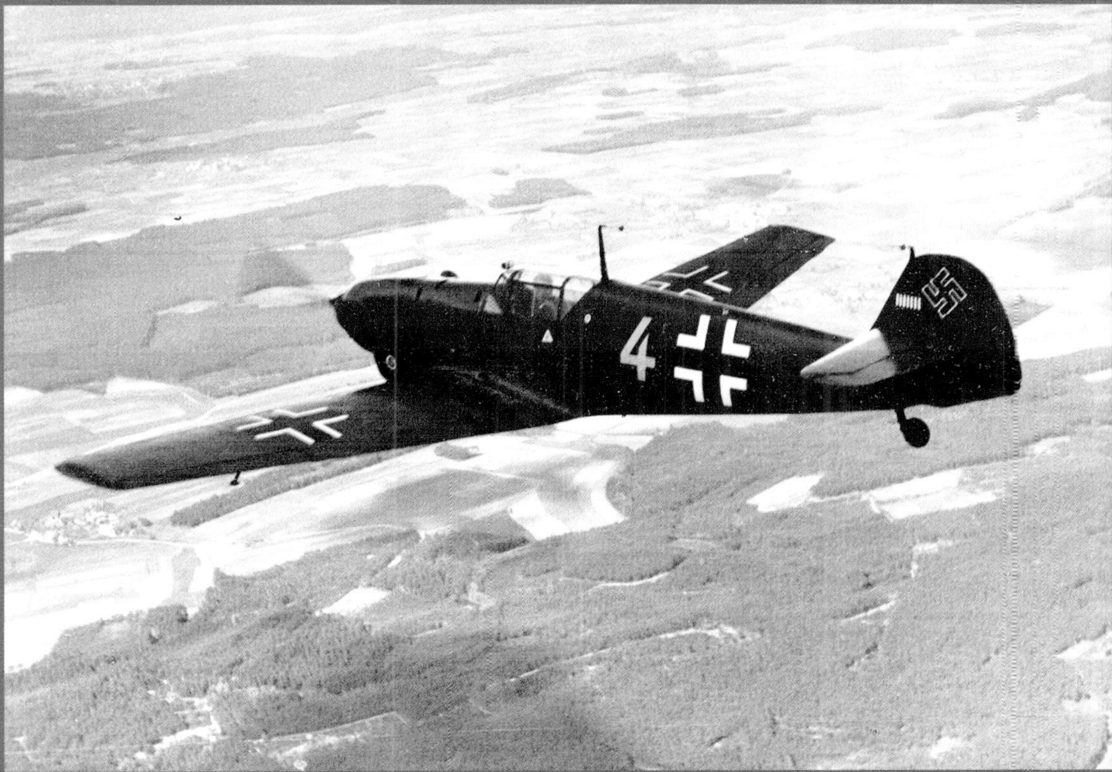

These two views are as unusual as they are mysterious. The seven victory bars on the tail correspond to Gentzen's victory tally, but they have been repainted lower down and the code "Yellow 4" is not that of the first Luftwaffe ace ... This Bf 109D-1, whose windscreen has been fitted with a rearview mirror, may therefore be his old aircraft after its withdrawal from the front and subsequent transfer to a training school.

Ground crew pose with the scoreboard of the *Kommandeur* of JGr. 102 painted on the tailfin of "Yellow 4."

Johannes Gentzen, one of the first Luftwaffe aces, was, exceptionally, not buried on site as was the case for most combatants. His fame and position meant that his body would be transferred back to the Reich. He still lies in Neubrandenburg cemetery.

Gentzen's victories

No	Date	Time	Aircraft	Unit	Place
1	Sep 2, 1939	1800	PZL P-23		S Radomsko
2	Sep 3, 1939	1040	PZL P-23		8km NE Radomsko
3	Sep 13, 1939	1015	PZL-37		Jaroslaw
4	Sep 14, 1939	1700	PZL P-23		
5	Sep 14, 1939	1700	PZL P-23		
6	Sep 14, 1939	1700	PZL P-23		
7	Sep 14, 1939	1700	PZL P-23		
8	Nov 8, 1939	1435	M.S.406		5km NE Edenkoben
9	Apr 4, 1940		Curtiss H-75	GC I/5	Beaumont-en-Argonne

Hptm. Johannes Gentzen—first ace of the Luftwaffe—with his men.

The wreckage of Gentzen's Bf 110C on May 26, 1940, at the edge of the airfield at Neufchâteau.

Major Kurt Ubben

Kurt "Kuddel" Ubben was born in Dorstadt in the Harz on November 18, 1911. His father was a naval officer, a branch of the armed forces which was probably the least impacted service from the limitations imposed after 1918 on the Wehrmacht by the Treaty of Versailles. The young man followed his father's career from 1931 onward. He was thus a pupil on the famous training ship *Gorch Fock*. But, in 1934, when military aviation was re-established, he joined the Luftwaffe—although theoretically a sailor, since he was assigned to naval aviation, initially flying with the Küstenjagdstaffel Kiel.

During this period the Kriegsmarine initiated the construction of its first aircraft carrier, the *Graf Zeppelin*. Even before its completion, an aviation group of two *Staffeln* was assigned to the carrier. Trägergruppe 186 (186th Carrier Wing) included 4./186, equipped with the Ju 87As and Bs, as well as 6./186, on the Bf 109C, established from 4./136 in Jever. Ubben flew as *Oberfeldwebel* in the fighter unit before being transferred to 5./186 created in July 1939. In Kiel-Holtenau, pilots practiced taking off and landing on a dummy flight deck.

On the eve of the Polish campaign, all available aircraft were deployed and the two naval air arm fighter *Staffeln* were thus posted to Brüsteort. After six days of the campaign in Poland and some 30 missions without incident, both 5. and 6. Staffeln were recalled to the West to be based in Hage, reinforcing the defense of the German Bight. From then on, operations comprised tiresome patrols and escorts, often over the sea.

During the campaign in the West, Tr.Gr. 186 operated over the Netherlands as part of Luftflotte 2. On May 10, 1940, attacks on the Dutch airfields of De Kooi and Texel took place. Ofw. Ubben achieved his first victory downing a Fokker D.21 fighter. On May 24, the *Gruppe* flew from Deurne (Antwerp) to Dunkirk before returning to Jever on June 2.

A II./186 (T) ground crewman poses in front of a Bf 109B displaying the insignia of the *Gruppe*: the arms of the family of Count Zeppelin. The unit was to operate from the aircraft carrier *Graf Zeppelin*.

Ofw. Ubben's Bf 109E-1 "Yellow 13" in the early spring of 1940, with the insignia of 6./Tr.Gr. 186: a witch on a broomstick. Ubben seems to have favored the number 13.

Kristiansand airfield. Pilots of 5./186 (T) during a short stay in Norway in June/July 1940. From left: Ofw. Kurt Ubben, Ofw. Hans-Wilhelm Schopper, Fw. Herbert Perrey, Lt. Täut, Lt. Teuschle (Heinz Deuschle?), Oblt. Lorenz "Papa Schulz" Weber (*Staffelkapitän*), Fw. Herbert Höhne (later called "Kaiser"), Fw. Helmut Bouillon (killed on February 18, 1942), and Fw. Reinhold Schmetzer (killed on May 7, 1944).

Berislav airfield (USSR), early September 1941. Oblt. Ubben on his return from a combat sortie in front of his Bf 109F-4 "Black 13" decorated with 36 victory bars. "Kuddel" would lead 8./JG 77 for several more weeks.

With work on *Graf Zeppelin* being delayed, if not suspended, II./186 reduced to two *Staffeln*, was renamed III./JG 77. An attempt was made to re-equip it with Curtiss H-75 fighters captured from the French Air Force. This experiment was a failure and the new III./JG 77 shifted to Brittany with Bf 109 "Emils." On July 22, 1940 Ubben, promoted to officer, took command of 8./JG 77.

The *Gruppe* remained on the defensive in France until shortly before the launch of Operation *Marita*, the invasion of the Balkans. On April 19, 1941 over Larissa, *Staka* Ubben scored his second

October 1, 1941. Ubben claimed his 40th victory, downing an I-16 of the 32 IAP, while the rudder of his "Black 13" clearly indicates the award of the Knight's Cross. This close-up allows us to identify the first two successes, in the Netherlands and Greece. It should be noted that his 22nd claim would not be confirmed, so his score was in fact 39.

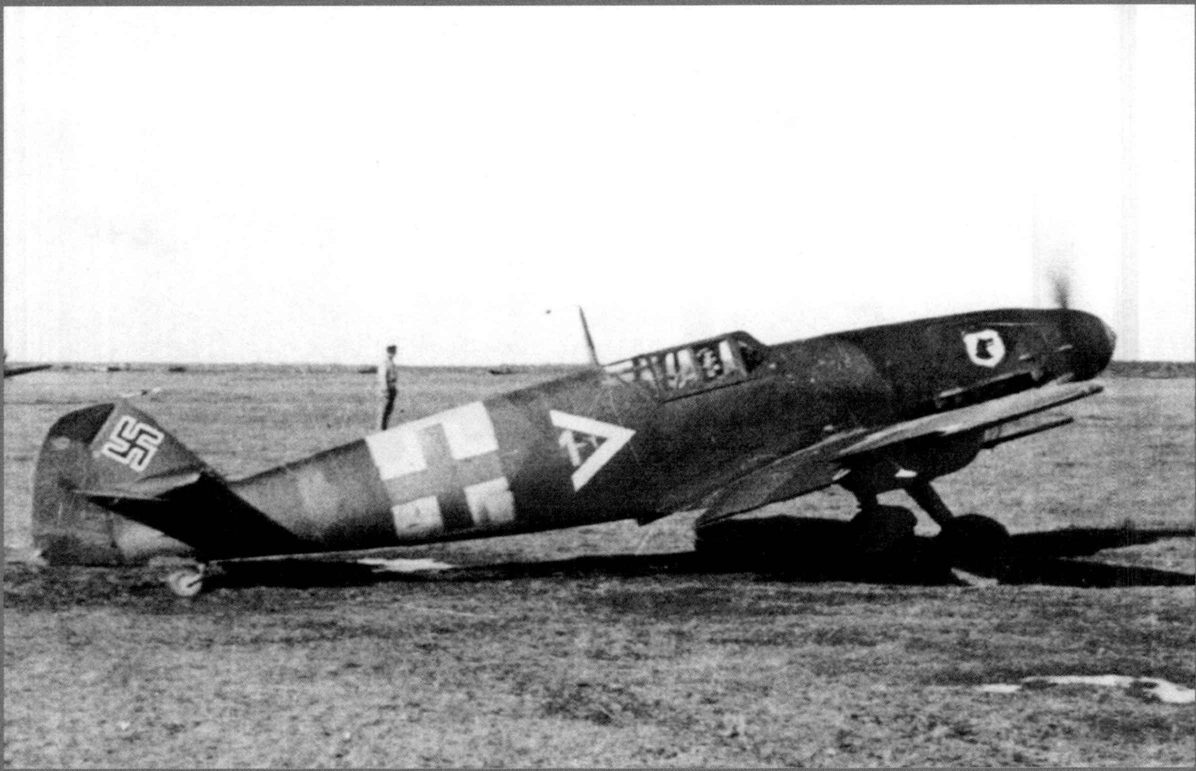

Ubben's Bf 109G-2 in its R6 "gunboat" configuration at Nikolskoye in early September 1942. At this time the ace had claimed 88 victories. His aircraft is not displaying the usual "double chevron" of a *Gruppenkommandeur*, but a simple "chevron 1."

In view of its somewhat itinerant existence, the *Kommandeur* of III./JG 77 adapted the *Gruppe* badge—taken from the coat of arms of the previous commander Alexander von Winterfeldt—by adding the inscription "*Wander-Zirkus Ubben*" ("Ubben's travelling circus"). Humor and irony are combined here on the side of this Bf 109G-6 Trop. This is the only occasion in the history of the Tagjagd that the name of the *Gruppenkommandeur* appeared in full on the aircraft of his unit.

In Sicily, after the abandonment of Tunisia, Ubben (left) confers with Kommodore Steinhoff (back to camera) and another great ace, the fighter inspector for the South, Günther Lützow.

victory, downing a Hurricane of No. 33 Squadron but was himself a victim of anti-aircraft fire. He had to land his Bf 109E-7 W.Nr. 5198 at Doblatan, about 20 kilometers from his lines before being picked up by the *Gruppe* liaison Fi 156, his comrades having done their utmost to extricate him from this dangerous situation. During Oeration *Merkur*, Ubben and his men took part in attacks on shipping around Crete. Operating in the fighter-bomber role, he claimed one bomb dropped on the battleship *Warspite* on May 22 and was credited with sinking a patrol boat the next day.

In the opening days of *Barbarossa* the invasion of the USSR, Ubben's score rose rapidly. He flew multiple sorties against the waves of Soviet medium bombers launched without escort and in an almost suicidal manner on the German columns, in a largely vain attempt to slow their advance. It is obvious that many of these victories are not verifiable, but it was equally the case that the Soviet Air Force was bled dry during these "pigeon shoots." Such sorties were not without danger for the attackers, subjected as they were to crossfire from Soviet machine-gunners.

On September 5, 1941, "Kuddel" Ubben was awarded the Knight's Cross for 32 victories (plus he had already returned four more by that date). Shortly afterwards, he took command of III./JG 77, handing over 8. Staffel to his comrade, Oblt. Emil Omert.

The fighting in the East continued despite the harsh winter of 1941/2. On March 12, 1942, Hptm. Ubben received the Knight's Cross with Oak Leaves at Adolf Hitler's HQ.

At the end of 1942, JG 77 left for Africa to replace JG 27, which had been bled dry. Kurt Ubben thus took part in the retreat from Libya, which saw the *Geschwader* holed up in the Axis bridgehead in Tunisia. During the period leading up to the evacuation from Africa in early May 1943, he added a further 14 victories.

Appointed *Kommodore* of JG 2, Major Ubben flew his first sorties in the Fw 190 in the early spring of 1944.

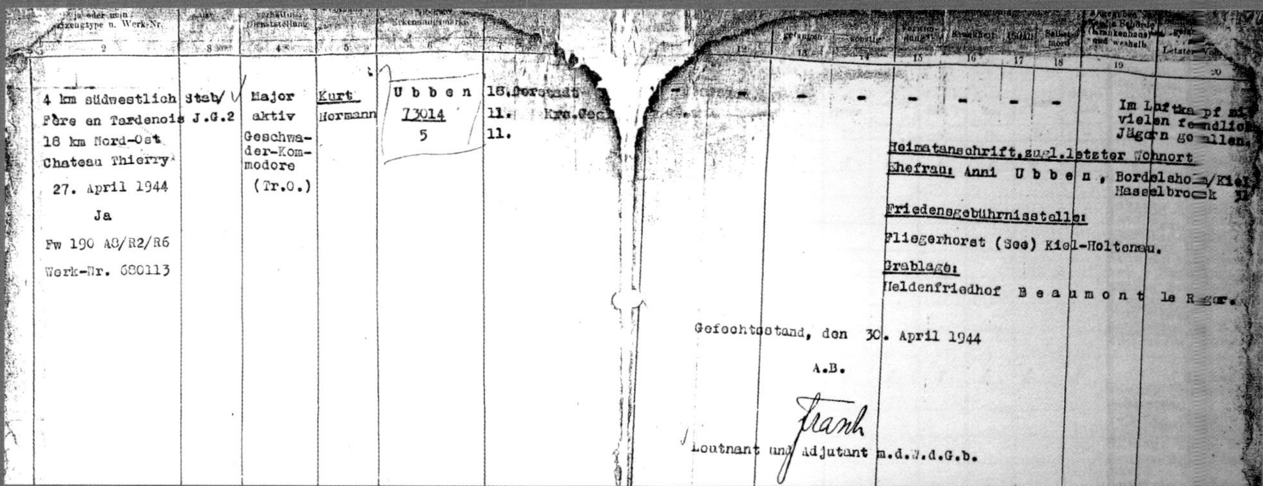

4 km südwestlich Fère en Tardenois 18 km Nord-Ost Chateau Thierry
27. April 1944
Ja
Fw 190 A8/R2/R6
Werk-Nr. 680113

Stab/ J.G.2

Major
aktiv
Geschwader-Kommodore
(Tr.O.)

Kurt
Hermann

U b b e n
73014
5

18.
11.
11.

Im Luftkampf mit vielen feindlichen Jägern gefallen.

Heimatanschrift, zugl. letzter Wohnort
Ehefrau: Anni U b b e n, Bordesholm/Kiel
Hasselbrook

Friedensgebührnisstelle:
Fliegerhorst (See) Kiel-Holtenau.

Grablage:
Heldenfriedhof B e a u m o n t le R[illegible].

Gefechtsstand, den 30. April 1944

A.B.

Frank

Leutnant und Adjutant m.d.W.d.G.b.

Verlustmeldung (loss report) for Kommodore Ubben. His Fw 190A-8 W.Nr. 680113 crashed four kilometers southwest of Fère-en-Tardenois, 18 kilometers northeast of Château-Thierry.

Based for a while in Sardinia, III./JG 77 came up against P-38 fighters escorting bomber formations attacking the island. Kommandeur Ubben added three of these Lightnings to his victory scoreboard. There then followed the retreat through continental Italy via Corsica. A Beaufighter was claimed departing the island of Corsica. The ace won his 110th official victory a week later, during an interception sortie against the U.S. Twelfth Air Force bombers, his victim being a B-17 on its way to Augsburg. At the end of October, Ubben was temporarily assigned to lead JG 53, a unit that had seen its previous *Kommodore* (himself an interim appointee) "at the end of his rope." This one-month internship was to prepare him for other duties.

At the end of 1943, decimated and almost at the end of its resources, III./JG 77 deployed to Romania to take over from I./JG 4 which replaced III./JG 77 in the north of Italy. There followed a brief respite, enabling the *Gruppe* to rest and refit. On March 10, 1944, Hptm. Ubben was promoted to *Major* and was posted to France to take over command of JG 2, succeeding Egon Mayer who had been killed in action. The ace had to convert onto the Fw 190, having previously only flown the Messerschmitt Bf 109 (from the "Berta" through the "Gustav"). These changes in operational fronts and aircraft would prove fatal for Ubben. On April 27, on only his third combat flight at the head of Jagdgeschwader 2, he was shot down and killed by USAAF P-47s at Saponay. "Kuddel" Ubben, originally buried in the "Richthofen" cemetery of honor at Beaumont-le-Roger, now lies in the German military cemetery of Saint-Désir-de-Lisieux next to his unfortunate predecessor Egon Mayer.

Major Kurt Ubben was credited with 111 victories in more than 500 combat flights, as well as a patrol boat and 15 tanks.

Ubben's victories

No	Date	Time	Aircraft	Unit	Place
1	May 10, 1940	0650	Fokker D XXI		Kooi
2	Apr 19, 1941	1120	Hurricane	33 Sqn	25km N Lamia
3	Jun 22, 1941	1858	I-16		Bessarabia
4	Jun 26, 1941	1045	DB-3		Black Sea Romanian coast
5		1045	DB-3		
6		1102	DB-3		
7		1447	DB-3		
8	Jul 4, 1941	1608	SB-3		Bessarabia
9		1837	SB-3		
10	Jul 8, 1941	1823	DB-3		Bessarabia
11		1830	DB-3		
12		1837	DB-3		
13	Jul 10, 1941	1113	I-153		SE Balti
14		1115	I-153		
15		1118	I-153		
16	Jul 11, 1941	1239	MiG-3		Bessarabia
17	Jul 21, 1941	1238	I-61		S Ukraine
18	Jul 22, 1941	1232	I-61		S Ukraine

19	Jul 25, 1941	1940	I-153	66 ChAP	S Ukraine
20		1943	I-153	66 ChAP	
21	Jul 27, 1941	1542	I-153		S Ukraine
-	Jul 27, 1941		I-16		S Ukraine
22	Jul 31, 1941	1253	I-16		S Ukraine
23		1700	Potez XXV ?		
24	Aug 5, 1941	1755	I-16		S Ukraine
25		1803	I-16		
26	Aug 11, 1941	1548	I-16		S Ukraine
27	Aug 13, 1941	0848	I-15		S Ukraine
28	Aug 17, 1941	1705			Seversky S Ukraine
29	Aug 22, 1941	1100	I-15		60km WSW Kherson
30	Aug 29, 1941	0705	DB-3		W Tchaplinka
31	Aug 30, 1941	1845	I-153		Dniepropetrovsk
32	Sep 1, 1941	1741	DB-3		Berislav
33		1753	I-16		
34	Sep 2, 1941		Pe-2		Berislav
35	Sep 4, 1951	0555	DB-3		Kiev
36	Sep 5, 1951	0535	I-16		Kiev
37	Sep 26, 1951	1600	I-153		Perekop
38	Sep 29, 1951	1102	R-10		Perekop
39	Oct 1, 1941		I-16	32 IAP	Perekop
40	Oct 2, 1941	1152	MiG-3		Perekop
41	Oct 3, 1941	1430	MiG-3		Perekop
42		1508	MiG-3		
43	Oct 9, 1941	1512	MiG-3		NW Tokoultchak
44		1516	MiG-3		
45	Oct 10, 1941	0615	Il-2		Perekop
46		0630	Mig-3		
47	Oct 11, 1941	1405	Pe-2		S Perekop
48	Oct 18, 1941		LaGG-3		Tchaplinka
49	Oct 19, 1941	1252	LaGG-3		Tchaplinka
50		1612	I-15		
51	Oct 20, 1941	1608	LaGG-3		SW Jouchoum
52	Oct 22, 1941	0910	Il-2		Perekop
53	Oct 23, 1941	1625	I-15	8 IAP/ChF	Perekop
54	Nov 4, 1941	1508	I-153		Crimea

55	Nov 6, 1941		Mig-3		Crimea
56			Il-2		
57	Dec 7, 1941	1410	I-15		Crimea
58	Dec 9, 1941	0905	DB-3		Crimea
59		1230	I-15		
60		1233	I-15		
61		1235	I-15		
62	Dec 11, 1941	1333	SB-2		Crimea
63	Dec 31, 1941	1042	I-153		Crimea
64	Jan 7, 1942	0910	Pe-2		NE Feodosia
65	Feb 24, 1942		LaGG-3		E Feodosia
66	Mar 2, 1942	0930	Il-2		NE Feodosia
67	Mar 5, 1942		I-16		NE Feodosia
68	Mar 9, 1942	1255	I-153		NE Feodosia
69	Mar 12, 1942		I-153		Crimea
70	Mar 17, 1942	1234	DB-3		N Feodosia
71	May 12, 1942	1710	Il-2		Tchougouiev
72	May 27, 1942	1522	Pe-2		NW Isjum
-	Jun 8, 1942		I-153		Sevastopol
-	Jun 11, 1942		Il-2		Sevastopol
-	Jun 12, 1942		LaGG-3		Sevastopol
73	Jun 18, 1942	0400	LaGG-3		SE Alma Tamak
74		1508	I-153		Sevastopol
75	Jun 24, 1942		Yak-1	6 GvIAP/ChF	Sevastopol
76	Jul 1, 1942	1710	Yak-1		Crimea
77	Jul 2, 1942	1444	Il-2		Bagerowo
78	Jul 5, 1942		Yak-1		Crimea
79		1720	Il-2		Kerch/Tamar
80		1723	Il-2		
81	Jul 6, 1942	1852	Yak-1		Kerch/Tamar
82			LaGG-3		
83	Jul 9, 1942	1112	Yak-1		Kerch
84	Jul 14, 1942	1728	I-16		Crimea
85	Jul 22, 1942	0952	Yak-1		Taganrog
-	Sep 9, 1942		Il-2		

-	Sep 10, 1942		Yak-1		
86	Sep 12, 1942	1401	Pe-2		65km E Sloboda
-	Sep 14, 1942		Il-2		
87	Sep 15, 1942	0711	LaGG-3		NE Voronezh
88	Sep 16, 1942	0744	Yak-1		ENE Kantemirovka
-	Sep 20, 1942		P-40		
-	Sep 20, 1942		LaGG-3		
89	Sep 21, 1942	1115	Pe-2		60km E Sloboda
-	Sep 22, 1942		LaGG-3		
-	Sep 25, 1942		Yak-1		
90	Sep 26, 1942	1452	LaGG-3		ENE Kantemirovka
91	Sep 30, 1942	1130	Yak-1		ENE Kantemirovka
92	Nov 3, 1942	1410	P-40		SW El Daba
93	Nov 5, 1942	1430	Hurricane	274 Sqn	W Fuka
94	Nov 7, 1942	1620	P-40	250 Sqn	Sollum
95	Dec 11, 1942	0940	P-40	66th FS/57th FG	W Marsa el Brega
96	Dec 13, 1942	1300	P-40	66th FS/57th FG	E Nofilia/Merduma
97	Dec 15, 1942	1055	P-40	260 Sqn	nr Ras Al Ali
98	Jan 10, 1943	0840	P-38		W Wadi Tamet
99	Jan 13, 1943	0845	P-40		Bir Dufan
100	Jan 14, 1943	1115	P-40	3 Sqn RAAF or 250/450 Sqn	SW Zliten
101		1625	P-40	3 Sqn RAAF	S Bir el Gheddahia
102	Jan 27, 1943	1550	P-40		Mejdez el-Bab
103	Feb 4, 1943	1510	P-38F	1st or 82nd FG	SW El Guettar
104	Feb 8, 1943	1249	P-38G	82nd FG	W Cekhira/S Sened
105		1301	P-38G		
106	Feb 15, 1943	1201	Spitfire		30km SW Sidi Bou Zid
107	May 6, 1043	1050	P-38	350th FG	10–15km Cape Bon
108	Jun 24, 1943	0955	P-38	1st FG	W Bosa/SW Oristano
109		1015	P-38	1st FG	
-	Aug 10, 1943		P-38		Sardinia
-	Sep 25, 1943		Beaufighter		NE Porto-Vecchio
110	Oct 1, 1943	1155	B-17F 42-30053	352nd FS/301st BG	nr Metato
111	Oct 21, 1943	1135	P-38		SW Grosseto

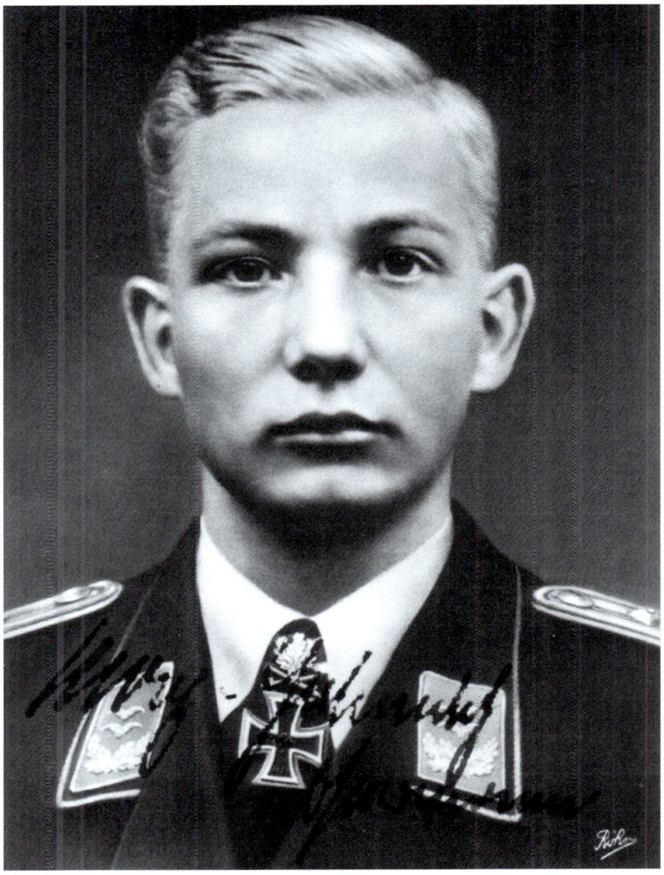

Oblt. Max-Hellmuth Ostermann was awarded the Knight's Cross with Oak Leaves and Swords (no. 10) on his 100th *Abschuss*, May 12, 1942. He was on leave at the time, having wounds treated in his right thigh and forearm.

Oberleutnant Max-Hellmuth Ostermann

Max-Hellmuth was born on December 11, 1917, in Hamburg. He was the only son of August, who worked in the Justice Department, and Emma (née Albers) Ostermann. After graduating from school and being attracted to aviation, he volunteered for the Luftwaffe in March 1937. After attending several aviation schools, he obtained his pilot's licence and the rank of *Leutnant* at the end of 1939. He was then sent to Düsseldorf to I./ZG 1, a *Zerstörer* unit. He was so small that his mechanics had to fix wooden blocks on the rudder pedals to enable him to reach them! Uncomfortable with the heavy fighter Bf 110, he was sent to a *Staffel* flying the Bf 109, 1./JG 21, in Mönchen-Gladbach on April 7, 1940. On May 10, I./JG 21 took part in the offensive in the West with its 46 Bf 109 "Emils" (of which 34 were serviceable), first over Belgium, before reaching Charleville and then Signy-le-Petit. On May 20, Lt. Max-Hellmuth Ostermann claimed a Morane of GC I/6 west of Péronne. Two victims are known: Sgt Duchêne-Marulaz, hit by shrapnel from an incendiary shell, who had to land at high speed in a field, gear up, and Sgt Pagès, burnt, who bailed out. Six days later, scrambled from Monchy-Breton, close to Saint-Pol, a score of

Maintenance being carried out on Lt. Ostermann's Bf 109F-2 "White 2" during the summer of 1941.

Lt. Max-Hellmuth Ostermann conferring with pilots and mechanics of 7. Staffel, with the Knight's Cross awarded on September 5, 1941. "Little Max" had won 29 victories by that stage.

Ostermann proudly poses in front of the rudder of his Bf 109F-2 while his mechanics update his record: 40 claims as of September 7, 1941. However, he had to wait until October 30, 1941 for his 40th certified victory, downing a 175 ChAP Il-2 during a Soviet raid against Siverskaya airbase.

On April 4, 1942, at the Wolfsschanze (Wolf's Lair), the Führer personally presented the 81st Oak Leaves to Oblt. Max-Hellmuth Ostermann. Note he has kept on his leather gloves. Hptm. Kurt Ubben, Kommander of III./JG 77, received the same decoration while Hptm. Hans Philipp (left) became just the eight Luftwaffe airman to be awarded the Knight's Cross of the Iron Cross with Oak Leaves and Swords.

Messerschmitts of I./JG 21 were attacked from the rear by 12 machines from GC III/1 and five from GC I/4 close to Cambrai. Ostermann shot down the Curtiss of Lt André Stiquel (GC I/4), but part of the wing of his Bf 109 was torn off by the tail of his opponent.

On June 23, I./JG 21 passed under the command of Stab/JG 54 at Soesterberg (Netherlands) in view of the forthcoming offensive against England. I./JG 21 was at that point redesignated 7./JG 54. On August 12, 1940, while JG 54 was patrolling with other *Jagdgruppen* in the Folkestone–Dungeness sector to open the way for the Dornier Do 17 Z bombers of I./KG 2, the young second lieutenant Ostermann was credited with the Spitfire Mk I piloted by Flt Lt Brian Smith of No. 610 Squadron. The RAF pilot bailed out.

On August 30, during a raid on Biggin Hill, Max defeated a Spitfire of No. 222 Squadron but on September 1, he had to make a forced landing at Saint-Inglevert, his Bf 109E-3 W.Nr. 1647 "White 11" having been slightly damaged in air combat. Six days later, he obtained the status of ace (five victories) by defeating a Hurricane near Ashford. On September 30, as the Luftwaffe committed its fighters in numbers over London, he shot down another No. 222 Squadron Spitfire over Tonbridge, Kent, probably FS Iain Hutchinson's P9492 that came down at Denham.

On October 8, JG 54 sortied to cover 11 Bf 109 fighter-bombers over London. On the way back, the formation was attacked by Spitfires from No. 72 Squadron and Hurricanes from No. 303 (Polish) Squadron. Hurricane Mk I "RF-R" (R4175) of Sgt Josef Frantisek, the RAF pilot with the most victories in the battle of Britain, crashed near Sutton on the outskirts of London. It is likely that the victor over the Czech ace was the young Max-Hellmuth Ostermann. The latter also shot down a Spitfire from No. 74 Squadron near Maidstone on October 20. This was his last victory against an RAF fighter, his sixth during the battle of Britain.

On April 6, 1941, during Operation *Marita*, he surprised an Me 109E-3 of the 102 Esk; the Yugoslav fighter ("White L-55" of Warrant Officer Karlo Štrbenk) crashed 15 kilometers north of Belgrade, near the village of

Glognjski. Unlike this aircraft, the IK-2 he claimed the next day was not confirmed.

During *Barbarossa*, his successes in the sky accumulated. On July 6, Ostermann shot down two SB-2 bombers of the 41 SAD, his 19th and 20th confirmed successes. On August 1, 1941, he shot down a DB-3—the "Green Hearts" 1,000th victory. On the same day, his squadron leader was wounded in action. Ostermann temporarily took the position of *Staffelkapitän* of 7./JG 54 until the return of Günther Scholz on September 18. Under his leadership, 7. Staffel won 41 victories between August 2 and September 17. On September 4, 1941, he was awarded the Knight's Cross by General Alfred Keller for his 29 victories; he was the eighth pilot in JG 54 to receive this decoration. Promoted to *Oberleutnant* on October 29, he was transferred to 3./JG 54 at the beginning of November 1941 and assumed the duties of acting *Staffelführer* for one month. The "Ostermann effect" was not long in

Oblt. Ostermann as he closes in on 100 victories. The winter flight suit is still de rigueur in late April/ early May 1942, even though the white camouflage of the Bf 109F-4 W.Nr. 13114 "Black 1" of the ace has partially faded.

In combat with "Ratas" on May 10, 1942, Oblt. Ostermann was badly shot up. The ace managed to belly-land his Bf 109F-4 W.Nr. 13088 "Black 1" in German lines, but the tail of the aircraft was almost torn off in the crash-landing. The rudder bears a representation of the Oak Leaves awarded for 62 victories. Below it are his next 35 victories achieved in this aircraft.

coming, with several pilots of 3. Staffel immediately emerging from the shadows. He claimed his 50th *Abschuss* ("shoot-down") on January 9, 1942, and proved to be an excellent leader as well as fighter. In February 1942, he married his fiancée, Anneliese. Cutting short his leave to return to the front, he was entrusted with 8./JG 54 on March 14, 1942. As was the case during his time with 3. Staffel, his drive spurred on the "*Piepmatz*" ("cheeky sparrow") *Staffel*. Previously, he had received the Oak Leaves (March 12) for his 62nd confirmed aerial success. From March 14 to 31, he scored a further 20 confirmed victories (nos. 63 to 82) at the controls of the Bf 109F-4 "Black 1." He also increased the number of aircraft shot down by III./JG 54 to 500. He sortied farther and farther behind Soviet lines. On May 10, he took off in Bf 109F-4 (W.Nr. 13088) "Black 1" for a *Freie Jagd*, a free hunt, over the Liuban pocket, accompanied by Gefr. Gerhard Dietz. Shot down by a Polikarpov, his Messerschmitt made an emergency landing in the German lines. Soldiers from the Heer helped Ostermann to extricate himself from his cockpit. Two days later, on May 12, 1942, he shot down two I-16s, returning his 100th victory, but, wounded by shrapnel during the mission, he made another emergency landing and was transported to the Siverskaya Lazarett. Repatriated to continue his treatment, he returned to the East on July 31, 1942. III./JG 54 was then based in Relbitsy. However, this *Draufgänger* (daredevil) fell victim to his excessive recklessness on August 9, 1942. On that day, he was in combat with P-40s near Amossovo, far behind enemy lines. He did manage to put a P-40 out of action, his 102nd victory. However, he did not see the LaGG-3 piloted by Lt Arkadiy Soukov of the 41st IAP slide into a firing position behind his Bf 109G-2 W.Nr. 10438 "Black 1." His machine was hit hard, made several uncontrolled maneuvers and finally crashed east of Lake Ilmen. Ostermann's death was probably one of the greatest losses sustained by the Tagjagd according to some. In 300 combat sorties, he had returned 102 credited victories, eight of which were in the West. Major Hannes Trautloft, *Kommodore* of the JG 54, wrote about this virtuoso pilot: "There is always talk of 'irreplaceable loss' and that 'nothing will be the same afterwards.' It is true that we continued to fly and fight after Ostermann's death, but I never again found this breed of fighter in my Geschwader."

The tailfin of Max-Hellmuth Ostermann's Bf 109F-4/R1 W.Nr. 13114 "Black 1" decorated with 100 victories, at Siverskaya airfield on May 12, 1942. It was one of the two personal aircraft assigned to the young *Staka* of 8./JG 54.

Ostermann's victories

No	Date	Time	Aircraft	**Unit**	**Place**
1	May 20, 1940	1820	MS.406		W Péronne
2	May 26, 1940	0906	H-75	GC I/4	Arras
3	Aug 12, 1940	0935	Spitfire	610 Sqn	nr Ashford
4	Aug 30, 1940	1905	Spitfire	222 Sqn	nr Ashford
5	Sep 5, 1940	1040	Hurricane		Ashford
6	Sep 30, 1940	1437	Spitfire	222 Sqn	Tonbridge
7	Oct 8, 1940	1146	Hurricane	303 Sqn	S London
8	Oct 8, 1940	1538	Spitfire	74 Sqn	SE London
9	Apr 6, 1941	1243	Bf 109E-3		Belgrade
-	Apr 7, 1941		IK-2		
10	Jun 23, 1941	1151	SB-2	9th BAP	Kedainiai area
11		1158	SB-2	9th BAP	
12	Jun 24, 1941	1832	SB-2		Daugavpils
13	June 30, 1941	1210	DB-3	57th BAP	Daugavpils
14		1212	DB-3	57th BAP	
15		1215	DB-3	57th BAP	
16	Jul 5, 1941	2004	SB-3	41st SAD	Over river Velikaya
17		2006	SB-3		
18		2008	SB-3		
19	Jul 6, 1941	1735	SB-3	41st SAD	
20		1737	SB-3	41st SAD	
21	Jul 28, 1941		MiG-3	402nd IAP	Ostrov
22	Aug 1, 1941	1906	DB-3		NW Luga
-	Aug 10, 1941		2 × I-18 (MiG-3)		
-	Aug 12, 1941		I-16		
23	Aug 14, 1941	1701	I-153	71st IAP	Narva Bay
24		1704	I-153	71st IAP	Narva Bay
25	Aug 17, 1941	1137	I-16		SW Leningrad
26	Aug 18, 1941	0525	I-16		Leningrad area
27		1102	I-16		Leningrad area
28	Aug 21, 1941	1045	I-18 (Mig-3)		Mga
29	Aug 23, 1941	0803	I-16		E Narwa
-	Sep 4, 1941		I-16		
30	Sep 5, 1941	1545	I-16		nr Leningrad
31	Sep 7, 1941	1425	I-18 (MiG-3)	44th IAP	Shlisselburg
32		1430	I-18 (MiG-3)	44th IAP	

33	Sep 8, 1941	1725	I-18 (MiG-3)		Demyansk area
34	Sep 10, 1941	1024	I-26 (Yak-1)		Demyansk area
35	Sep 11, 1941	0751	I-15		Demyansk
36		1012	SB-3		Staraïa Rousa
-	Sep 12, 1941		DB-3191st IAP		
37	Sep 17, 1941	1024	I-18 (MiG-3)		Krasnoïe Selo
-	Sep 23, 1941		assault plane		
-	Oct 7, 1941		I-18 (MiG-3)		
38	Oct 25, 1941	1415	I-26 (Yak-1)		
39	Oct 29, 1941	1350	I-26 (Yak-1)		Tikhvine
40	Oct 30, 1941		Il-2	175th ChAP	N Mind
41	Nov 13, 1941	1504	Pe-2	125th BBAP	Leningrad
42	Nov 16, 1941	1516	I-26 (Yak-1)		Leningrad
43		1520	I-26 (Yak-1)		
44	Nov 19, 1941	0635	Douglas PS-84	GVF	Komendanstkoye airfield
45	Nov 30, 1941	1345	Douglas PS-84	GVF	Komendanstkoye airfield
46	Dec 1, 1941	1510	I-26 (Yak-1)		NE Leningrad
47	Jan 1, 1942	1237	Tomahawk	158th IAP	Zelenets island
48	Jan 8, 1942	1242	Tomahawk	158th IAP	Leningrad
49		1350	Tomahawk	158th IAP	
50		1515	Yak-1		
51	Jan 11, 1942	1505	I-18 (MiG-3)		Leningrad
52	Jan 20, 1942	1412	I-26 Tomahawk	154th IAP	Leningrad area
53	Jan 23, 1942	1103	I-16		Leningrad area
54		1127	Il-2		Leningrad area
55	Jan 24, 1942	1307	I-16		Leningrad area
56	Jan 25, 1942	1045	MBR-2 (MP-1)		Lake Ladoga
57		1112	I-153	71st IAP	
58		1126	I-153	71st IAP	
59	Jan 26, 1942	1321	Pe-2		Leningrad area
60	Jan 28, 1942	0918	I-15		Leningrad area
61		1501	I-18 (MiG-3)	159th IAP	nr Volkhov
62	Feb 1, 1942	1050	Curtiss P-40	158th IAP	Leningrad
63	Mar 14, 1942	1707	I-26 (Yak-1)		Leningrad area
64	Mar 16, 1942	0826	I-26 (Yak-1)		Leningrad area
65	Mar 17, 1942	1006	I-18 (MiG-3)		Leningrad area
66		1400	RZ		E Volkhov
67		1403	RZ		

<table>
<tr><td>68</td><td rowspan="2">Mar 18, 1942</td><td>1635</td><td>Curtiss P-40</td><td></td><td rowspan="2">Leningrad area</td></tr>
<tr><td>69</td><td>1702</td><td>biplane</td><td></td></tr>
<tr><td>70</td><td rowspan="2">Mar 19, 1942</td><td>1115</td><td>Curtiss P-40</td><td></td><td rowspan="2">Leningrad area</td></tr>
<tr><td>71</td><td>1142</td><td>I-18 (MiG-3)</td><td></td></tr>
<tr><td>72</td><td rowspan="2">Mar 20, 1942</td><td>1221</td><td>I-18 (MiG-3)</td><td></td><td rowspan="2">Leningrad area</td></tr>
<tr><td>73</td><td>1721</td><td>RZ</td><td></td></tr>
<tr><td>74</td><td>Mar 21, 1942</td><td>1140</td><td>I-18 (MiG-3)</td><td></td><td>Leningrad area</td></tr>
<tr><td>75</td><td rowspan="2">Mar 22, 1942</td><td>1743</td><td>I-18 (MiG-3)</td><td></td><td rowspan="2">Leningrad area</td></tr>
<tr><td>76</td><td>1755</td><td>I-18 (MiG-3)</td><td></td></tr>
<tr><td>77</td><td>Mar 28, 1942</td><td>1014</td><td>I-18 (MiG-3)</td><td></td><td>Leningrad area</td></tr>
<tr><td>78</td><td rowspan="3">Mar 29, 1942</td><td>0928</td><td>I-16</td><td></td><td rowspan="3">Leningrad area</td></tr>
<tr><td>79</td><td>1157</td><td>I-18 (MiG-3)</td><td></td></tr>
<tr><td>80</td><td>1205</td><td>I-18 (MiG-3)</td><td></td></tr>
<tr><td>81</td><td rowspan="2">Mar 31, 1942</td><td>1315</td><td>I-18 (MiG-3)</td><td></td><td rowspan="2">Leningrad area</td></tr>
<tr><td>82</td><td>1333</td><td>I-18 (MiG-3)</td><td></td></tr>
<tr><td>83</td><td>Apr 1, 1942</td><td>1812</td><td>I-18 (MiG-3</td><td></td><td>Leningrad area</td></tr>
<tr><td>84</td><td rowspan="3">Apr 23, 1942</td><td>1230</td><td>MiG-3</td><td></td><td rowspan="3">Lake Ladoga</td></tr>
<tr><td>85</td><td>1230</td><td>MiG-3</td><td></td></tr>
<tr><td>86</td><td>1602</td><td>MiG-3</td><td></td></tr>
<tr><td>87</td><td>Apr 24, 1942</td><td>0641</td><td>RZ</td><td>662nd NBAP</td><td>Leningrad area</td></tr>
<tr><td>88</td><td>Apr 25, 1942</td><td>1130</td><td>I-180 (Yak-7)</td><td></td><td>nr Cronstadt</td></tr>
<tr><td>89</td><td rowspan="2">Apr 27, 1942</td><td>0615</td><td>Curtiss P-40</td><td></td><td>Leningrad area</td></tr>
<tr><td>90</td><td>1818</td><td>Curtiss P-40</td><td></td><td>Bol'tchaya Roudka</td></tr>
<tr><td>91</td><td rowspan="2">Apr 29, 1942</td><td>1622</td><td>MiG-3</td><td></td><td rowspan="2">Leningrad area</td></tr>
<tr><td>92</td><td>1625</td><td>MiG-3</td><td></td></tr>
<tr><td>93</td><td rowspan="2">Apr 30, 1942</td><td>1341</td><td>Curtiss P-40</td><td></td><td rowspan="2">Leningrad area</td></tr>
<tr><td>94</td><td>1406</td><td>MiG-3</td><td></td></tr>
<tr><td>95</td><td rowspan="2">May 6, 1942</td><td>1812</td><td>I-180 (Yak-7)</td><td></td><td rowspan="2">Leningrad area</td></tr>
<tr><td>96</td><td>1819</td><td>I-180 (Yak-7)</td><td></td></tr>
<tr><td>97</td><td>May 7, 1942</td><td>0558</td><td>Curtiss P-40</td><td></td><td>Leningrad area</td></tr>
<tr><td>98</td><td>May 9, 1942</td><td>1523</td><td>Curtiss P-40</td><td></td><td>N Lake Ilmen</td></tr>
<tr><td>-</td><td>May 10, 1942</td><td>0825</td><td>I-180 (Yak-7)</td><td></td><td>nr Boudogotch</td></tr>
<tr><td>99</td><td rowspan="2">May 12, 1942</td><td>0936</td><td>I-16</td><td></td><td>ENE Tosno/Liouban area</td></tr>
<tr><td>100</td><td>0941</td><td>I-16</td><td></td><td>ENE Tosno/Liouban area</td></tr>
<tr><td>101</td><td>Aug 8, 1942</td><td>1858</td><td>Curtiss P-40</td><td></td><td>nr Amosovo</td></tr>
<tr><td>102</td><td>Aug 9, 1942</td><td>1133</td><td>Curtiss P-40</td><td></td><td>NW Krestzy</td></tr>
</table>

Oberst Hermann Graf

Hermann Graf was born on October 24, 1912, in Engen im Hegau. He divided his leisure time between soccer and gliding, while pursuing a brilliant education. Volunteering for the Lufwaffe, he joined JG 51 in 1939 and then rather reluctantly became an instructor. Fortunately, he joined the 9./JG 52 in the summer of 1940 and established a reputation as a master tactician and fighter virtuoso. On August 4, 1941, he achieved his first *Abschuss* and formed a "team" with Alfred Grislawki, Ernst Süss, and Heinrich Füllgrabe, known as the "Schwarm Graf." During October this foursome inflicted heavy losses on Soviet assault aircraft pummeling German infantry. Graf had 42 victories by the end of 1941 and was awarded the Knight's Cross on January 24, 1942. On March 23 of that year, he became the new *Kapitän* of 9./JG 52. On May 2, 1942, Graf notched up seven confirmed victories (nos. 70–76) over the Crimea and learnt the same evening that he had been awarded the Knight's Cross with Oak Leaves. On May 14, he became the seventh fighter pilot in history to achieve 100 aerial victories. Ten days later, he was summoned to the Führer's headquarters for his Knight's Cross with the Swords while he was still only a *Leutnant*. On September 4, during the fighting over Stalingrad, Graf reached his 150th *Abschuss*. On September 15, the ace received a personal telegram of congratulations from Reichsmarschall Göring for his 172 victories, a figure which earned him promotion to *Hauptmann* and the Knight's Cross with Oak Leaves, Swords, and Diamond, until then an award given to only four airmen. In just six weeks, Hptm. Hermann Graf shot down 75 enemy aircraft in the Stalingrad sector. After a long leave of absence, he was commissioned by Göring to create a special unit to counter RAF Mosquitoes: the Jagdgruppe Süd, renamed Jagdgeschwader 50.

Seen here at Kharkov-Rogan (Ukraine) in early 1942, Fw. Grislawski was photographed with his *Schwarmführer*'s Bf 109F-4 "Yellow 1" as a backdrop. Graf had achieved around 50 victories at this time.

Mechanics of 9./JG 52 paint the latest victory markings on the tailfin of Kapitän Hermann Graf's Bf 109F-4 "Yellow 1" at Kharkov-Rogan airfield in May 1942.

Seen on May 14, 1942 at Kharkov-Rogan, there are 104 victories marked up on the tail of Graf's Bf 109 F-4 (W.Nr. 7420).

JG 50 was initially equipped with eight Messerschmitt Bf 109G-5s and Bf 109G-6s fitted with the GM-1 engine power-boosting system. Graf chose a further three aces, Oblt. Alfred Grislawski, Obfw. Ernst Süß, and Fw. Heinrich Füllgrabe, from his old *Staffel*, the 9./JG 52, for the new unit. Ultimately, both JG 50 (and its sister unit Jagdgeschwader 25) were particularly unsuccessful in countering the Mosquito but enjoyed comparatively more success intercepting U.S. heavy bomber formations during the daylight offensive over Europe in 1943/4.

JG 50 was one of the first formations to use the Werfer-Granate 21 rocket mortar operationally, with one carried under each wing. While these rockets could bring down a bomber with one hit, they were designed to disperse the tightly packed bomber formations rather than as a direct-fire weapon. On July 31, 1943, the unit was declared operational, with a total of 19 aircraft. On August 17, 1943, the unit intercepted American bomber forces attacking the Messerschmitt factory in Regensburg and the ball-bearing plants in Schweinfurt. Grislawski claimed two Boeing B-17 Flying Fortresses downed on this raid. On September 6, the unit shot down four Flying Fortresses over Stuttgart, one to Grislawski, and two claimed by Graf with the WGr. 21, before Graf was then shot down but survived a forced landing. Grislawski claimed one other kill with the unit, a B-17, on October 14. By October, JG 50 had been disbanded. Graf was subsequently appointed *Kommodore* of JG 11 in November 1943, a unit engaged in the defense of the Reich. Six four-engine aircraft and three USAAF P-51s fell to his guns. He was subsequently posted back to JG 52 at the end of September 1944 as *Kommodore*. He totalled 212 victories at that time—this being his final score. Wounded on March 29, 1944, in combat with P-51s of the 4 FG, his left arm continued to suffer. As a result, he was no longer able to fly. At the time of the capitulation of May 1945, Graf (then with the JG 52 in Czechoslovakia) was delivered with his comrades to the Soviets. He

Kapitän Hermann Graf at the controls of his Bf 109G-2 "Yellow 1." Note the red heart of the Karaya Staffel with the inscription "Inge."

Pitomnik, September 15, 1942. Graf's terrier Roland greets his master whose score now stands at 172 victories.

Graf tops 150 aerial victories.

Eleven days later. In downing three Soviet aircraft over Stalingrad on September 26, 1942, Hptm. Hermann Graf became the first pilot in history to exceed 200 aerial victories.

Hermann Graf flew at least two colourful Fw 190As during his time with JGr.Ost. Fw 190A-5 W.Nr. 2594 (seen here) featured a yellow engine cowling decorated with a tulip pattern and was fitted with "high-altitude ram intakes."

would be repatriated at the end of 1949. The fact that he very quickly became a member of the Komite Freies Deutschland, a puppet organization manipulated by Stalin, and that he received favorable treatment for this fact, would make him very unpopular with his ex-comrades, who would treat this great ace as a virtual outcast until the end of his life. Stricken by Parkinson's disease, Hermann Graf died in his hometown on November 4, 1988.

Graf's victories

No	Date	Time	Aircraft	**Unit**	**Place**
1	Aug 4, 1941	0620	I-16		nr Kiev
2	Aug 5, 1941	0620	I-16		nr Kiev
3	Aug 11, 1941	1435	MiG-3		nr Kanev
4	Aug 30, 1941	0840	DB-3	4 BAK/DBA	nr Djnepopetrovsk
5	Sep 6, 1941	1823	I-16		nr Kremenschug
6	Sep 13, 1941	1046	Yak-1	VVS ChF	nr Perekop
7	Sep 24, 1941	1210	DB-3	52 DBAD	Balaklya
8	Sep 27, 1941	1422	DB-3	8 BAP	nr Kharkov
9	Oct 3, 1941	1700	Yak-1		nr Kharkov
10		1705	I-16		
11	Oct 11, 1941	0710	SB-2		Lozovaya
12		0715	I-153		
13	Oct 14, 1941	1610	Yak-1		nr Valki
14		1613	Yak-1		
15	Oct 24, 1941	1250	MiG-3		Boysovka
16		1252	MiG-3		
17	Oct 25, 1941	1521	MiG-3	32 IAP	Aibary
18	Oct 27, 1941	1538	MiG-3		Yushno
19	Oct 28, 1941	1002	MiG-3		Aibary
20		1003	R-5		

21	Nov 1, 1941	1615	MiG-3		nr Sebastopol
22	Nov 8, 1941	1158	MiG-3		nr Rostov
23	Nov 9, 1941	1435	I-16		nr Shakty
24	Nov 11, 1941	1435	MiG-3		nr Rovenkiy
25	Nov 17, 1941	1438	I-16		nr Rostov
26	Nov 20, 1941	1352	Su-2		nr Agrafenovka
27	Nov 23, 1941	1336	Il-2	4 ShAP	nr Rostov
28	Nov 29, 1941	1021	I-16		Rostov
29		1027	U-16	DBA	
30		1307	Di-16		
31	Dec 2, 1941	1219	I-16		Taganrog
32	Dec 6, 1941	1252	Il-2	4 ShAP	Lysogorskaya
33		1425	I-16		nr Azov
34		1432	I-16		
35	Dec 8, 1941	0943	I-5		Taganrog
36		0944	I-5		
37		0952	I-16		nr Rabowka
38	Dec 27, 1941	1201	I-16	88 IAP	Taganrog and Ascb
39		1205	I-16	88 IAP	
40		1425	I-16		
41		1430	SB-2		Golodayevka
42	Dec 28, 1941	1332	Yak-1		Taganrog
43	Jan 7, 1942	1450	I-16		Sansoje
44		1455	I-16		Novaya Slobodka
45	Jan 8, 1942	1125	unidentified		Prilepiye
46	Jan 25, 1942	1542	I-16		nr Isjum
47	Feb 3, 1942	0935	Su-2	135 BAP or 13 GBAP	Nuvo
48	Mar 23, 1942	1306	Yak-1	135 BAP or 13 GBAP	Bniliza
49		1314	Yak-1		Burluk
50		1726	Su-2		Kotovka
51	Mar 25, 1942	0625	Yak-1		Staryi Saltov
52	Mar 27, 1942	1011	Yak-1		Volschansk
53		1718	MiG-3		Burluk
54	Mar 28, 1942	0553	Yak-1		Burluk
55		0618	MiG-3		Kotovka
56		17:8	MiG-3		Gniliza
57		1741	I-16		Stary Saltov
58	Mar 30, 1942	1205	MiG-3		Burluk
59	Apr 6, 1942	0602	I-16		nr Staryi Saltov
60		0604	I-16		
61	Apr 29, 1942		I-16	247 IAP	Kerch Peninsula
62			I-16	247 IAP	
63			I-15	247 IAP	
64	Apr 30, 1942		I-15		Kerch Peninsula
65			I-15		
66			I-15		
67		1642	Yak-1		
68		1647	Yak-1		
69		1650	Yak-1		

<table>
<tr><td>70</td><td rowspan="7">May 2, 1942</td><td>0400</td><td>I-16</td><td></td><td rowspan="7">Kerch Peninsula</td></tr>
<tr><td>71</td><td>0400</td><td>I-16</td><td></td></tr>
<tr><td>72</td><td>0400</td><td>I-16</td><td></td></tr>
<tr><td>73</td><td>1115</td><td>I-153</td><td></td></tr>
<tr><td>74</td><td>1115</td><td>MiG-3</td><td></td></tr>
<tr><td>75</td><td></td><td>MiG-3</td><td></td></tr>
<tr><td>76</td><td></td><td>MiG-3</td><td></td></tr>
<tr><td>77</td><td>May 3, 1942</td><td></td><td>I-16</td><td></td><td>Crimea</td></tr>
<tr><td>78</td><td>May 5, 1942</td><td></td><td>MiG-1</td><td></td><td>Crimea</td></tr>
<tr><td>79</td><td rowspan="8">May 8, 1942</td><td></td><td>MiG-1</td><td></td><td rowspan="8">Crimea/Kerch</td></tr>
<tr><td>80</td><td>1058</td><td>MiG-1</td><td></td></tr>
<tr><td>81</td><td>1102</td><td>MiG-1</td><td></td></tr>
<tr><td>82</td><td>1107</td><td>I-15</td><td></td></tr>
<tr><td>83</td><td></td><td>I-15</td><td></td></tr>
<tr><td>84</td><td>1332</td><td>I-15</td><td></td></tr>
<tr><td>85</td><td>1728</td><td>I-15</td><td></td></tr>
<tr><td>86</td><td></td><td>MiG-3</td><td></td></tr>
<tr><td>87</td><td rowspan="2">May 9, 1942</td><td></td><td>Yak-1</td><td></td><td rowspan="2">Crimea</td></tr>
<tr><td>88</td><td></td><td>Yak-1</td><td></td></tr>
<tr><td>89</td><td rowspan="2">May 11, 1942</td><td></td><td>I-16</td><td></td><td rowspan="2">Kerch Peninsula</td></tr>
<tr><td>90</td><td></td><td>I-16</td><td></td></tr>
<tr><td>91</td><td>May 12, 1942</td><td></td><td>I-16</td><td></td><td>Kharkov</td></tr>
<tr><td>92</td><td rowspan="6">May 13, 1942</td><td></td><td>MiG-1</td><td></td><td rowspan="6">Kharkov area</td></tr>
<tr><td>93</td><td></td><td>MiG-1</td><td></td></tr>
<tr><td>94</td><td></td><td>MiG-1</td><td></td></tr>
<tr><td>95</td><td></td><td>MiG-1</td><td></td></tr>
<tr><td>96</td><td></td><td>MiG-1</td><td></td></tr>
<tr><td>97</td><td></td><td>LaGG-3</td><td></td></tr>
<tr><td>98</td><td rowspan="7">May 14, 1942</td><td></td><td>MiG-1</td><td></td><td rowspan="7">Kharkov/Staryi Saltov/ Kotovka</td></tr>
<tr><td>99</td><td></td><td>MiG-1</td><td></td></tr>
<tr><td>100</td><td></td><td>Su-2</td><td></td></tr>
<tr><td>101</td><td>1645</td><td>Su-2</td><td></td></tr>
<tr><td>102</td><td>1645</td><td>Pe-2</td><td></td></tr>
<tr><td>103</td><td>1645</td><td>R-10</td><td></td></tr>
<tr><td>104</td><td>1645</td><td>I-16</td><td></td></tr>
<tr><td>105</td><td>May 16, 1942</td><td></td><td>MiG-1</td><td></td><td>Kharkov</td></tr>
<tr><td>106</td><td>May 20, 1942</td><td>1737</td><td>Su-2</td><td>99 BAP</td><td>Kharkov</td></tr>
<tr><td>107</td><td>May 22, 1942</td><td></td><td>LaGG-3</td><td></td><td>Kharkov</td></tr>
<tr><td>108</td><td>May 23, 1942</td><td>1628</td><td>I-16</td><td></td><td>Kharkov</td></tr>
<tr><td>109</td><td rowspan="3">Jun 30, 1942</td><td></td><td>Pe-2</td><td></td><td>Poltava</td></tr>
<tr><td>110</td><td></td><td>LaGG-3</td><td></td><td rowspan="2">Kharkov</td></tr>
<tr><td>111</td><td></td><td>LaGG-3</td><td></td></tr>
<tr><td>112</td><td>Aug 3, 1942</td><td>1830</td><td>Il-2</td><td>7 GShAP</td><td>Caucasus</td></tr>
<tr><td>113</td><td>Aug 5, 1942</td><td>0937</td><td>LaGG-3</td><td></td><td>Caucasus</td></tr>
<tr><td>114</td><td>Aug 12, 1942</td><td>1432</td><td>Yak-1</td><td></td><td>Caucasus</td></tr>
<tr><td>115</td><td>Aug 13, 1942</td><td>1532</td><td>I-16</td><td></td><td>Caucasus</td></tr>
</table>

116	Aug 14, 1942	1014	I-16		Kuban
117		1020	I-16		
118		1337	Yak-1		
119		1352	Hurricane		
120		1357	LaGG-3		
121	Aug 15, 1942	1641	Yak-1		Kuban
122	Aug 16, 1942	1654	I-16		Kuban
123	Aug 17, 1942	1142	I-153	238 ShAD	Kuban
124		1536	I-153	238 ShAD	
125		1541	I-153	238 ShAD	
126	Aug 18, 1942	1643	I-153	238 ShAD	Kuban
127		1643	R-5		
128	Aug 22, 1942	1355	Il-2	763 LBAP	Stalingrad area
129		1403	Yak-1		
130	Aug 23, 1942	0722	LaGG-3	527 IAP/864 IAP or 9 GIAP	Stalingrad area
131		0727	LaGG-3	8 VA	
132		1328	LaGG-3	527 IAP/864 IAP or 9 GIAP	
133		1331	I-180	527 IAP/864 IAP or 9 GIAP	
134	Aug 24, 1942	0928	I-180		Stalingrad area
135		0958	Il-2		
136	Aug 25, 1942	1151	Il-2	527 IAP/864 IAP or 9 GIAP	Stalingrad area
137		1727	LaGG-3	527 IAP/864 IAP or 9 GIAP	
138	Aug 29, 1942	1422	LaGG-3	527 IAP/864 IAP or 9 GIAP	Stalingrad area
139	Aug 30, 1942	1652	Pe-2	270 BAD	Stalingrad area
140		1707	Il-2		
141	Sep 2, 1942	0912	P-40	731 IAP	Stalingrad area
142		0915	P-40		
143		1332	Il-2	ADD	
144		1712	DB-7	527 IAP/864 IAP or 9 GIAP	
145		1715	LaGG-3	731 IAP	
146	Sep 3, 1942	1348	Yak-1		Stalingrad area
147		1351	Yak-1		
148		1706	Yak-1	527 IAP/864 IAP or 9 GIAP	
149		1713	LaGG-3	527 IAP/864 IAP or 9 GIAP	
150	Sep 4, 1942	1012	Yak-1		Stalingrad area
151	Sep 5, 1942	1650	P-40	629 IAP	Stalingrad area
152	Sep 6, 1942	1321	Yak-1		Stalingrad area
153		1323	Yak-1		
154		1327	Yak-1		
155	Sep 8, 1942	1128	La-5		Stalingrad area
156		1129	La-5	27 IAP	
157		1135	Il-2	206 ShAD	
158	Sep 9, 1942	1321	La-5	27 IAP	Stalingrad area
159		1334	La-5	287 IAD	
160		1646	LaGG-3	287 IAD	
161	Sep 10, 1942	1524	La-5	287 IAD	Stalingrad area
162		1535	La-5	287 IAD	
163	Sep 11, 1942	1558	Pe-2	270 BAD	Stalingrad area
164		1609	P-40	731 IAP	

165	Sep 12, 1942	1647	P-40	629 IAP	Stalingrad area
166		1713	P-40	629 IAP	
167	Sep 14, 1942	0800	I-16	629 IAP	Stalingrad area
168		0804	I-16	629 IAP	
169		0809	Yak-1	629 IAP	
170	Sep 15, 1942	0635	I-153	629 IAP	Stalingrad area
171		0639	I-16	629 IAP	
172		0705	LaGG-3	527 IAP/864 IAP or 9 GIAP	
173	Sep 16, 1942	0735	P-40	731 IAP	Stalingrad area
174		0739	Su-2	270 BAD	
175	Sep 17, 1942	0848	Yak-1		Stalingrad area
176		0852	Yak-1		
177		1436	LaGG-3	527 IAP/864 IAP or 9 GIAP	
178	Sep 18, 1942	1137	LaGG-3	527 IAP/864 IAP or 9 GIAP	Stalingrad area
179		1159	LaGG-3	527 IAP/864 IAP or 9 GIAP	
180		1212	Il-2	228 ShAD or 291 ShAD	
181	Sep 20, 1942	0820	LaGG-3	527 IAP/864 IAP or 9 GIAP	Stalingrad area
182	Sep 21, 1942	1132	Yak-1		Stalingrad area
183		1140	Yak-1		
184		1625	Yak-1		
185		1702	Il-2		
186	Sep 22, 1942	1120	I-16	629 IAP	Stalingrad area
187		1645	Yak-1		
188	Sep 23, 1942	1042	Yak-1		Stalingrad area
189		1103	Yak-1		
190		1105	Yak-1	527 IAP/864 IAP or 9 GIAP	
191		1107	Yak 1	527 IAP/864 IAP or 9 GIAP	
192		1430	LaGG-3		
193		1431	LaGG-3	270 BAD	
194		1433	LaGG-3	270 BAD	
195		1639	Yak-1		
196		1642	Yak-1		
197		1655	LaGG-3	527 IAP/864 IAP or 9 GIAP	
198	Sep 25, 1942	1441	La-5	278 IAD	Stalingrad area
199		1446	La-5	278 IAD	
200	Sep 26, 1942	0857	I-153	629 IAP	Stalingrad area
201		1642	LaGG-3	527 IAP/864 IAP or 9 GIAP	
202		1658	LaGG-3		
203	June 1943		Mosquito		Groningen
204	end July 1943	1050	B-17		
205	Sep 6, 1943	1108	B-17		Stuttgart/Black Forest
206			B-17		
207	Feb 10, 1944	1150	B-17		S Celle
208	Feb 24, 1944	1340	B-24		Grissen
209	Mar 6, 1944		B-24	453rd BG	E Berlin
210	Mar 8, 1942		P-51		nr Celle
211	Mar 29, 1944		P-51	4th FG	Hanover
212			P-51	4th FG	Schwarmstedt

Oberstleutnant Hans Philipp

Born in Meissen on March 17, 1917, Hans Philipp thought of becoming a journalist but finally joined the Luftwaffe in April 1935. He was promoted to *Leutnant* on February 24, 1938; however, at the end of his training, his potential went unrecognized. He was transferred to a bomber unit but did not like it and joined the *Jagdfliegerschule* (fighter flying school) at Werneuchen on May 1, 1938. Following the Anschluss, he was transferred to Vienna-Aspern with I./JG 138 which became 1./JG 76.

On October 13, 1940, Oblt. Hans Philipp (center) has just returned his 16th, 17th, and 18th official victories. He is seen relaxing on the field at Campagnelès-Guines in the company of the technical officer of JG 54, Oblt. Werner Pichon Kalau von Hofe (with cap) and an unidentified officer.

The rudder of Oblt. Hans Philipp's "Emil" after his 21st official victory on October 30, 1940: a Canadian Spitfire shot down near Lydd.

Philipp's "White 9," probably at Sarudin in late July 1941. The aircraft's rudder displays 46 victory markings.

The tail of Hans Philipp's "Friedrich" in early August 1941, with his two dachshunds, Löwe and Minke-Pinke, on the starboard horizontal stabilizer.

An interesting view from a *Propaganda Kompanie* report (August 6, 1941) showing Hans Philipp with a record of 50 victories. Note that the details of the seven victories in France (first line) do not quite correspond with what we know of his record. Similarly, the ace's rudder records 16 victories during the battle of Britain, whereas only 15 were credited to him. The seven bars without a roundel on the last line do not correspond with anything known; they perhaps mark the impatience of the painter towards his "boss" who has not "scored" for a week. He would very soon make up for it.

In Poland, he scored his first victory on September 5, 1939: a PZL.11 in the Lodz region.

Philipp claimed his second victory in the Western campaign on May 18, 1940: an H-75 of GC I or II/4 near Rethel (but only one or two damaged aircraft are known). Another followed on May 19. This time, no less than nine "M.S.405s" were claimed west of Laon by 1. Staffel, whereas the Armée de l'Air only lost three M.S.406s over the Aisne region that day. On Friday, May 24, 1940, over Dunkirk, "Fips" came up against the RAF for the first time and claimed a Spitfire. He then had to wait until June 3 to officially become an ace, shooting down two Curtiss H-75As of GC I/5 between Reims and Épernay. On the evening of Friday, June 7, the brand-new ace shot down a "Spitfire," probably a Hurricane of No. 43 Squadron, south of Dieppe. The next day he claimed his eighth victory, downing a Bloch 151.

Promoted to *Oberleutnant*, he took over 4./JG 54 on August 25, 1940. On October 22, he was awarded the Knight's Cross for 20 victories. For the first day of combat in the USSR, June 21, 1941, JG 54 claimed 45 victories. Oblt. Hans Philipp shot down a Tupolev SB-2 bomber northwest of Kovno (Kaunas), in Lithuania. He repeated this five days later in the Dünaburg (Daugavpils) sector, Latvia, and then scored a hattrick of Ilyushin DB-3s on June 30. On August 13, II./JG 54 faced for the first time aircraft of the Baltic Air Fleet (VVS KBF). "Fips" was credited with five enemy fighters (his 53rd–57th successes). On August 19, 4./JG 54 had a total of 200 *Luftsiegen*; no other *Staffel* had ever achieved such a figure. Kapitän Philipp, who now claimed 63 victories, having shot down two fighters the day before and three on the day itself, was the first JG 54 ace, and the 33rd soldier in the German armed forces to be awarded the Oak Leaves.

Hans Philipp was promoted to *Hauptmann* on November 18 and in February 1942 took command of I./JG 54. On March 31, he reached the milestone of 100 aircraft shot down. He then flew to the Führer's headquarters where he received his Swords. A short spell of leave followed. In the summer of 1942, the ace fell victim to dysentery and had to be hospitalized in Königsberg. Transferring to the Fw 190A-4, Kommandeur Philipp reached 150 victories on January 14, 1943, and became the second fighter pilot in history to reach the 200-victory mark, on March 17, shortly after being appointed *Major*. This apparent ease masked an unfailing concentration.

Rudder decoration of Philipp's Bf 109F-2 celebrates the Swords awarded on March 12, 1942.

On March 31, 1942, Philipp's F-2 (which was repainted with the regulation "double chevron" of a *Kommandeur*) was photographed displaying a symbol for 86 victories, plus 14 additional bars.

On April 1, 1943, he left the "Green Hearts" and was posted back to the West. The Luftwaffe needed experienced men to lead the defense of the Reich against the increasingly heavy raids mounted by the Eighth USAF. Promoted to *Kommodore* of JG 1, Philipp could not adapt to this change of front. For him, fighting 20 Soviet aircraft or Spitfires was still a sport where the best man won. In the USSR, dogfighting was still possible. On the other hand, combat against American four-engine "boxes" gave him the impression of running into a brick wall, especially given that German pilots were facing odds as much as 10 to 1. However, his experience enabled him to shoot down a Spitfire on May 2, 1943, then a P-47 on the 16th. On October 8, 1943, after having achieved his 206th victory, knocking down the only B-17 in his victory list, Philipp was jumped by a P-47 of the 61st FS/56th FG. Wounded in the face, he dove away and managed to bail out of his Fw 190A-6 only 50 meters from the ground. His lifeless body was found in a wood at Nordhorn with multiple fractures. He was buried six days later in Meissen in the presence of many senior Luftwaffe officials. According to Obstlt. Hannes Trautloft, Philipp had nothing of the Prussian soldier; he had a rather relaxed and carefree attitude. He never raised his voice to give an order. Despite his successes, he always maintained a friendly attitude, the mark of a great and endearing personality. His final tally was 206 victories (178 in the East, two in the Balkans and 26 on the Western Front).

Philipp's victories

No	Date	Time	Aircraft	Unit	Place
1	Sep 5, 1939	1415	PZL P.24 (PZL.11)	Eskadra Bombawa Lekka	7km S Radomsko
-	Sep 5, 1939	1415	PZL P.24		S Radomsko
2	May 18, 1940	1625	Curtiss H-75	GC II/4	W Rethel
3	May 19, 1940	1830	M.S.406		W Laon
4	May 24, 1940		Spitfire		Dunkerque/Calais
5	Jun 3, 1940	1520	Curtiss H-75		W Epernay
6		1525	Curtiss H-75		
7	Jun 7, 1940	2050	Spitfire	N°43 Sqn	S Dieppe
8	Jun 8, 1940		Bloch 151		
9	Aug 30, 1940		Hurricane		
10	Sep 1, 1940		Hurricane		
11	Sep 5, 1940	1620	Spitfire	N°41 Sqn	Thames estuary
12	Sep 27, 1940	1020	Hurricane		W London
13			Spitfire		
14			Spitfire		
15		1618	single seater		Hastings
16	Oct 13, 1940	1402	Hurricane		Dungeness/Tonbridge
17		1403	Hurricane		
18		1403	Hurricane		
19	Oct 20, 1940	1105	Hurricane	N° 602 Sqn	New Romney
20		1105	Hurricane		

21	Oct 30,1940	1702	Spitfire		Dungeness
22	Nov 2, 1940	1120	Spitfire	N°41 Sqn	NW Dungeness
23	Nov 14, 1940	1230	Hurricane	N°238 Sqn	Canterbury
24	Apr 7, 1941	1755	Bf 109E	32nd Yougoslav FG	S Neusatz
25		1803	Bf 109E		
26	Jun 22, 1941	1645	SB-2		NW Kovno
27	Jun 27, 1941	1945	SB-2		Dünaburg
28	Jun 30, 1941	1145	DB-3		Dünaburg
29		1512	DB-3		
30		1520	DB-3		
31	Jul 2, 1941	0830	I-16	2 SAD	Dünaburg
32		0832	I-18	2 SAD	
33		2013	SB-2		
34	Jul 6, 1941	1840	SB-2		Ostrow
35	Jul 8, 1941	1500	I-15		Ostrow
36		1512	I-15		
37	Jul 11, 1941	1710	SB-2		
38	Jul 12, 1941	2030	I-15		Lake Pesna/Porkhov
39	Jul 18, 1941	0900	I-18		
40		1455	I-18		
-			I-18		
41	Jul 20, 1941	1430	I-18		
42	Jul 21, 1941	1605	I-18		
43	Jul 22, 1941	1800	I-18		Gorolevo
44	Jul 30, 1941	0720	I-16		
45		0725	I-16		
46		1110	I-16		
47		1634	I-16		
48		1645	I-18		
-			I-16		
49	Aug 10, 1941	1020	I-18		Poretche
50		1600	I-16		
51	Aug 11, 1941	1325	I-16		
52		1445	I-16		
53	Aug 13, 1941	0920	I-18	VVS KBF	
54		0925	I-18	VVS KBF	
55		1355	I-18	VVS KBF	
56		1555	I-16	VVS KBF	
57		1800	I-16	VVS KBF	

58	Aug 18, 1941	1100	I-18		nr Krasnogvardeïsk
59		1105	I-18		
60	Aug 19, 1941	1250	I-16		nr Krasnogvardeïsk
61		1745	I-16		
62		1755	I-18		
63	Aug 21, 1941	1145	I-18		nr Krasnogvardeïsk
64	Aug 21, 1941	1525	I-16		
65		1535	I-16		
66	Sep 2, 1941	1435	I-16		Leningrad
67	Sep 14, 1941	1415	I-18		Leningrad
68		1420	I-18		
69	Oct 2, 1941	0635	I-18		
70		0640	I-18		
71	Oct 7, 1941	1540	I-18		Ladoga Lake
-			patrol boat		
72	Feb 6, 1942	1400	R-5		SW Malaïa Vichera
73		1408	R-5		
74	Feb 16, 1942	1030	I-18		Siverskaïa
75		1035	I-18		
76		1042	I-18		
77	Feb 17, 1942	1340	I-18		
78	Feb 19, 1942	1010	I-18		
79	Feb 22, 1942	1430	I-18		
80	Feb 23, 1942	0905	P-40		
81	Feb 26, 1942	1200	P-40		
82	Feb 27, 1942	0840	I-18		
83		0847	I-18	154 IAP	
84	Feb 28, 1942	0936	I-18		
85	Mar 12, 1942	0936	I-18		
86		0955	I-18		
87	Mar 15, 1942	1634	I-18		Volkov
88	Mar 18, 1942	1308	I-18		
89	Mar 22, 1942	1045	I-18		
90		1625	I-18		
91	Mar 28, 1942	0910	I-18		
92	Mar 29, 1942	0845	I-18		
93		0845	I-18		
94		1115	I-18		
95		1125	I-18		

96	Mar 29, 1942		P-40		
97			P-400		
98	May 30, 1942	1617	MiG-3		
99	Jun 6, 1942	1725	P-40		
100		1726	P-40		
101	Jun 11, 1942	2025	Yak-1		
102	Jun 12, 1942	2010	MiG-3		
103	Jun 15, 1942	2001	LaGG-3		
104		2002	LaGG-3		
105	Jun 26, 1942	0937	Il-2		
106		0944	LaGG-3		
107		1628	LaGG-3		
108	Jul 11, 1942	1948	P-40		SE Leningrad
109	Aug 2, 1942	1426	LaGG-3		SE Leningrad
110		1431	LaGG-3		N Pouchkine
111	Nov 3, 1942	1145	R-5		E Shlisselburg
112	Nov 7, 1942	0749	P-40		Ligovo
113	Nov 9, 1942	0708	Hurricane		E Ladoskoye
114		0715	Hurricane		
115	Dec 16, 1942	1125	Yak-1		Kobona
116		1135	MiG-3		Shlisselburg
117		1355	MiG-3		
118		1359	fighter		W Ladoskoye
119	Dec 29, 1942	1359	I-15	71 IAP	NW Cholm
120	Dec 30, 1942	0930	Il-2		Demyansk
121		0955	Il-2		
122		1000	LaGG-3		
123		1030	LaGG-3		
124		1100	LaGG-3		
125		1212	LaGG-3		
126					
127					
128	Jan 6, 1943	1245	Il-2		Demyansk
129		1250	Il-2		
130		1255	LaGG-3		

131	Jan 6, 1943	0920	Mustang		Pola
132		0922	LaGG-3		
133		0925	LaGG-3		
134		0929	LaGG-3		
135		0932	LaGG-3		
136	Jan 10, 1943	1245	Il-2		Otserki
137	Jan 12, 1943	1055	Il-2		Shlisselburg
138		1059	Il-2		
139		1105	Il-2		
140		1112	Il-2		
141		1116	I-16		
142		1120	I-16		
143		1405	Pe-2	73 BAP	
144	Jan 13, 1943	1345	LaGG-3		Shlisselburg
145		1403	LaGG-3		Poutilovo
146	Jan 14, 1943	0903	Il-2		Mga
147		0915	Il-2		N Poutilovo
148		1135	Hurricane		SW Shlisselburg
149		1136	Hurricane		
150		1155	LaGG-3		
151	Jan 15, 1943	1303	Il-2		SW Mga
152		1305	Il-2		
153	Jan 22, 1943	1302	LaGG-3		Mouja/Mga
154		1312	Il-2		
155		1315	Il-2		
156	Jan 23, 1941	1110	LaGG-3		Shlisselburg
157		1115	R-5		
158		1302	LaGG-3		
159		1305	LaGG-3		
160		1310	LaGG-3		
161		1314	La-5		
162	Jan 24, 1941	1056	I-153		Shlisselburg
163	Feb 11, 1943	0914	LaGG-3		NE Pouchkine
164	Feb 14, 1943		Il-2		N Tossno
165			Il-2		
166	Feb 19, 1943	1210	LaGG-3		NE Liouban
167		1215	LaGG-3		
168	Feb 21, 1943	0845	LaGG-3		Pouchkine
169		0906	Airacobra		Liouban

170	Feb 22, 1943	1508	Il-2		Shlisselburg
171		1525	Il-2		
172	Feb 23, 1943	0840	LaGG-3		Pouchkine/Liouban/ Tossno
173		0845	LaGG-3		
174		0849	Yak-1		
175		0903	Yak-1		
176		0908	Yak-1		
177		0916	Yak-1		
178		1102	LaGG-3		
179		1108	LaGG-3		
180	Feb 28, 1943	0935	MiG-3		Demyansk
181	Mar 7, 1943	0907	LaGG-3		Pola/Touleba
182		0810	LaGG-3		
183		0914	LaGG-3		
184		1150	La-5		Zaloutche
185		1432	Il-2		SE Parfino/Khodni/ Louka
186		1435	Il-2		
187		1437	Il-2		
188		1440	Il-2		
189		1442	Il-2		
190	Mar 14, 1943	1325	LaGG-3		Zaloutche
191		1332	P-40		NE Korovitchno
192	Mar 15, 1943	1530	LaGG-3		Korovitchno
193		1532	LaGG-3		Louka
194		1535	LaGG-3		Zaloutche
195	Mar 16, 1943	1043	Airacobra		Pola/Parfino
196		1046	LaGG-3		Staraïa Roussa
197		1049	LaGG-3		
198		1052	LaGG-3		
199		1056	LaGG-3		
200	Mar 17, 1943	1613	LaGG-3		Parfino/Korovitchno/ Khodni
201		1615	LaGG-3		
202		1617	LaGG-3		
203		1619	LaGG-3		
204	May 2, 1943	1943	Spitfire		W Harlem
205	May 16, 1943	1312	P-47		nr Zeebrugge
206	Oct 8, 1943	1528	B-17	339th BS/96th BG	SSE Vechta

Leutnant Walther Ohlrogge

Walther Ohlrogge was born in Bochum on January 15, 1909, and could be considered as "old" for a fighter pilot, which earned him the nickname "*Altmeister*" ("Old Master"). In May 1940, he was posted to 5./JG 3 but had to wait until the battle of Britain to claim his first and only victory over an RAF aircraft. However, he was himself shot down in the Channel in this dogfight and spent three hours adrift in his life raft.

Like many of his comrades, it was the launch of *Barbarossa* that allowed him to run up his score. On November 4, 1941, Fw. Ohlrogge was awarded the Knight's Cross for 39 victories.

In 1942, he flew into Sicily with his *Staffel* to operate over Malta but was restricted to bomber escort and ground-strafing sorties. An officer's training course followed in Werder before he was transferred to 9./JG 3 still fighting in the USSR. He distinguished himself again, but was very seriously wounded on September 5, 1942, and was hospitalized for 18 months. Considered unfit for front-line duties, Lt. Ohlrogge was sent as an instructor in March 1944 to the EJG Süd in Provence. In May 1944, he reportedly returned his last victories, downing two B-26s raiding the South of France. Shortly afterwards, the unit (redesignated 12./EJG 1) evacuated to the Reich. Ohlrogge was then to return to the East and claimed six AFVs knocked out which were included in his victory total. He was subsequently posted to JG 7 but did not achieve any *Luftsiegen* on the Me 262.

His scoreboard is a little confusing. Officially, he was credited with 77 victories, the majority of which can be confirmed from known losses. Walter Ohlrogge died on April 30, 2003.

Fw. Ohlrogge wearing his Knight's Cross awarded for 39 victories.

Photographed in Sicily in early March 1942 while II./JG 3 was operating over Malta, Walther Ohlrogge's rudder displays 43 victory bars. In reality, his 43rd was not credited until July so he had "only" 42 confirmed victories. Note the small roundel above his first victory bar—his only success against the RAF.

Ohlrogge with his Knight's Cross poses alongside his rudder scoreboard. (Collection J. Charita)

Ohlrogge's victories

No	Date	Time	Aircraft	Unit	Place
1	Aug 16, 1940	1320	Spitfire		Ashford
2	Jun 25, 1941	1950	I-16	VVS Southwestern Front	Novograd Volynski
3	Jun 30, 1941	-	unidentified		Ukraine
4	Jul 2, 1941	0830	I-17	VVS Southwestern Front	Ukraine
5		0930	I-153	VVS Southwestern Front	Ukraine
6		0933	I-153	VVS Southwestern Front	Ukraine
7	Jul 5, 1941	1310	SB-2	VVS Southwestern Front	Ukraine
8		1620	DB-3	VVS Southwestern Front	Ukraine
9		1620	DB-3	VVS Southwestern Front	Ukraine
10		1620	DB-3	VVS Southwestern Front	Ukraine
11	Jul 12, 1941	1745	DB-3	VVS Southwestern Front	Ukraine
12		1750	DB-3	VVS Southwestern Front	Kiev sector
13	Jul 16, 1941	1625	unidentified	VVS Southwestern Front	Kiev sector
14	Jul 25, 1941	1745	R-5	VVS Southwestern Front	Kiev sector

15	Aug 17, 1941	1325	R-5		Uman region
16		1830	R-5		Uman region
17		1833	R-5		Uman region
18		1838	R-5		Uman region
19		1845	I-16	88 IAP	Uman region
20	Aug 20, 1941	1238	I-16	88 IAP	Uman region
21	Aug 21, 1941	1530		Marine shipment	Dniepr
22		1535		Marine shipment	Dniepr
23	Aug 24, 1941	0625	V-11	210 ShAP	Ukraine
24		0625	V-11	210 ShAP	Ukraine
25		1755	R-5	VVS Southern Front	Ukraine
		1810		VVS Southern Front	Ukraine
26	Aug 26, 1941	1720	R-5	VVS Southern Front	Ukraine
27		1720	R-5	VVS Southern Front	Ukraine
28		1720	R-5	VVS Southern Front	Ukraine
29	Sep 12, 1941	1000	I-26		Krementchouk
30		1010	I-26		Krementchouk
31		1135	I-153	44 IAD	Krementchouk
32	Sep 13, 1941	0654	V-11		Kiev sector
33		0655	V-11		Kiev sector
34		0658	V-11		Kiev sector
35	Sep 20, 1941	1052	I-26		Kiev sector
36		1055	DB-3		Kiev sector
37	Sep 23, 1941	-	unidentified		Kiev sector
38	Sep 25, 1941	0723	I-26		Kiev sector
39	Oct 22, 1941	1622	I-61		Perekop
40		1635	I-61		Perekop
41	Oct 23, 1941	1615	I-61		Perekop
42		1632	I-15	I-153	Perekop
	June 24, 1942	1950		2VA	Izioum region
43	July 16, 1942	1705	DB-3	2VA	Rostov
44	Jul 18, 1942	1010	MiG-1	2VA	Rostov
45	Jul 22, 1942	0500	MiG-1	2VA	Rostov
46	Jul 24, 1942	1525	Il-2	2VA	Rostov

47	Jul 26, 1942	1225	Il-2	2VA	
48		-	Il-2	2VA	
49		0834	Il-2	2VA	
50		0836	Il-2	2VA	
51		0838	Il-2	2VA	
52		1225	MiG-1	2VA	
53		1235	MiG-1	2VA	
54		1542	MiG-1	2VA	
55	Jul 31, 1942	0635	Hurricane	438 IAP	W Peskovatka
56		1110	Il-2	2VA	Lipologovskiy
57	Aug 3, 1942	0655	Il-2	2VA	W Sapadkovska
58		0705	Il-2	2VA	NE Petkovatka
59	Aug 11, 1942		unidentified		Volgorad sector
60	Aug 17, 1942		unidentified		Volgorad sector
61	Aug 19, 1942	1143	LaGG-3	8 VA	Doubovka
62		1222	Dubovka	8 VA	E Fastov
63		1756	DVB-3		S Prudki
64		-	LaGG-3		
65	Aug 22, 1942	0945	Pe-2	8 VA	Satov
66	Aug 23, 1942	1240	LaGG-3		Stalingrad
67	Aug 24, 1942	1156	unidentified		Stalingrad
68	Aug 25, 1942	0940	unidentified	8 VA	N Stalingrad
69	Aug 27, 1942		unidentified		Don sector
70	Aug 28, 1942		MiG-1		Don sector
71			unidentified		Don sector
72	Aug 29, 1942	0850	unidentified		NW Achtuba
73	Aug 31, 1942		unidentified		Stalingrad sector
74	Sep 2, 1942	1710	unidentified	140 BAP	30km Stalingrad
75	Sep 5, 1942	0605	LaGG-3		E Stalingrad
76	May 1944		B-26		S France
77			B-26		

The rudder of Gerhard Köppen's Bf 109F-4 "White 4" seen at Kharkov-Rogan. This photograph was taken after his 72nd victory, on February 27, 1942.

Leutnant Gerhard Köppen

Gerhard Köppen was born on May 17, 1918, in Holzendorf (Markt Brandenburg). The future ace was destined to be a farmer but chose to volunteer for the brand-new Luftwaffe at the age of 18. His first posting was to KG 1 Hindenburg but he was selected for fighter pilot training during 1939. He did not join a front-line unit until October 1940 when he was posted to 7./JG 52, almost at the end of the battle of Britain. He had to wait for the launch of *Barbarossa* to make a name for himself by shooting down Soviet aircraft at a frenetic pace.

On December 18, 1941, he was awarded the Knight's Cross for his 40th victory, returned on November 16. On February 27, 1942, he became the 79th soldier in the German armed forces to receive the Oak Leaves for his victories 69–72 and the first NCO to be so honored. The young man returned from leave at the end of April. In a fortnight he shot down 12 enemy aircraft (nos. 73–84). But on May 5, 1942, his luck changed. After shooting down a MiG-1, Köppen attacked two Pe-2 bombers over the northern coast of the Kerch Peninsula. He was surprised by their defensive fire, which forced him to ditch in the Sea of Azov. Pursued by two enemy patrol boats, he started to swim to shore when suddenly Soviet artillery opened fire on his downed machine and the unprotected pilot went under in a matter of seconds. Twelve days before his 24th birthday, Gerhard Köppen was reported missing. He had 85 air victories and a destroyed Soviet gunboat on the Dnieper. His younger brother, Eckhardt (born 1924), who was killed on January 15, 1945, as a paratrooper in a "Hermann Göring" detachment, was posthumously awarded the Knight's Cross.

A mechanic of 8./JG 52 in front of the tail of Gerhard Köppen's Bf 109 in early 1942.

Köppen's victories

No	Date	Time	Aircraft	Unit	Place
1	Jun 24, 1941	0730	DB-3	VVS Southern Front	Constanza
2		0750	DB-3	VVS Southern Front	
3		0550	DB-3	VVS Southern Front	
4		0555	DB-3	VVS Southern Front	
5	Aug 2, 1941	0505	I-16	VVS Southern Front	Constanza
6	Aug 4, 1941	0505	I-16	VVS Southwestern Front	Kiev
7	Aug 6, 1941	1030	I-16	VVS Southwestern Front	Kiev
8	Aug 9, 1941	0535	SB-2	VVS Southwestern Front	SE Kiev
9		0548	SB-2	VVS Southwestern Front	
10	Aug 17, 1941	1854	SB-2	VVS Southern Front	E Kanev
11		1856	SB-2	VVS Southern Front	
12	Aug 19, 1941	0550	MiG-3	VVS Southern Front	Brovary
13	Sep 2, 1941	1210	V-11	VVS Southwestern Front	W Krement
14		1215	V-11	VVS Southwestern Front	
15	Sep 3, 1941	1300	I-153	VVS Southwestern Front	N.O. Dnepropetrovsk
16	Sep 14, 1941	1745	I-153	VVS Southwestern Front	Djnepopetrowsk

<table>
<tr><td>17</td><td>Sep 18, 1941</td><td>1745</td><td>I-16</td><td>VVS Southwestern Front</td><td>SW Kiev</td></tr>
<tr><td>18</td><td rowspan="3">Sep 24, 1941</td><td>0743</td><td>I-16</td><td>VVS Southwestern Front</td><td>nr Tshutov</td></tr>
<tr><td>19</td><td>0745</td><td>SB-2</td><td>VVS Southwestern Front</td><td>nr Tshutov</td></tr>
<tr><td>20</td><td>1210</td><td>SB-2</td><td>VVS Southwestern Front</td><td>-</td></tr>
<tr><td>21</td><td rowspan="2">Sep 26, 1941</td><td>1324</td><td>R-10</td><td>VVS Southwestern Front</td><td>Kharkov</td></tr>
<tr><td>22</td><td>1325</td><td>R-10</td><td>VVS Southwestern Front</td><td>Poltava</td></tr>
<tr><td>23</td><td>Sep 27, 1941</td><td>1038</td><td>DB-3</td><td>VVS Southwestern Front</td><td>Kharkov</td></tr>
<tr><td>24</td><td>Sep 28, 1941</td><td>1520</td><td>SB-2</td><td>VVS Southwestern Front</td><td>nr Poltava</td></tr>
<tr><td>25</td><td>Oct 2, 1941</td><td>0939</td><td>I-61</td><td>VVS Southwestern Front</td><td>nr Poltava</td></tr>
<tr><td>26</td><td rowspan="2">Oct 4, 1941</td><td>1200</td><td>R-10</td><td>VVS Southwestern Front</td><td rowspan="2">nr Walki</td></tr>
<tr><td>27</td><td>1240</td><td>R-10</td><td>VVS Southwestern Front</td></tr>
<tr><td>28</td><td rowspan="2">Oct 5, 1941</td><td>1633</td><td>R-10</td><td>VVS Southwestern Front</td><td rowspan="2">nr Mertschik</td></tr>
<tr><td>29</td><td>1636</td><td>R-10</td><td>VVS Southwestern Front</td></tr>
<tr><td>30</td><td>Oct 14, 1941</td><td>1410</td><td>V-11</td><td>VVS Southwestern Front</td><td>Poltava</td></tr>
<tr><td>31</td><td>Oct 23, 1941</td><td>1034</td><td>I-61</td><td>VVS ChF</td><td>Juschun</td></tr>
<tr><td>32</td><td rowspan="2">Oct 25, 1941</td><td>1520</td><td>I-51</td><td>VVS ChF</td><td rowspan="2">Juschun</td></tr>
<tr><td>33</td><td>1523</td><td>I-51</td><td>VVS ChF</td></tr>
<tr><td>34</td><td>Oct 28, 1941</td><td>0650</td><td>Pe-2</td><td>VVS ChF</td><td>Juschun</td></tr>
<tr><td>35</td><td>Oct 31, 1941</td><td>1601</td><td>I-61</td><td>VVS ChF</td><td>nr Simferopol</td></tr>
<tr><td>36</td><td>Nov 8, 1941</td><td>1140</td><td>I-61</td><td>VVS Southern Front</td><td>nr Azovl</td></tr>
<tr><td>37</td><td rowspan="2">Nov 9, 1941</td><td>1352</td><td>I-18</td><td>VVS Southern Front</td><td rowspan="2">Djankoy</td></tr>
<tr><td>38</td><td>1355</td><td>I-18</td><td>VVS Southern Front</td></tr>
<tr><td>39</td><td rowspan="2">Nov 19, 1941</td><td>1342</td><td>I-26</td><td>VVS Southern Front</td><td rowspan="2">Rostov</td></tr>
<tr><td>40</td><td>1343</td><td>I-26</td><td>VVS Southern Front</td></tr>
<tr><td>41</td><td>Nov 23, 1941</td><td>1338</td><td>Il-2</td><td>VVS Southern Front</td><td>Rostov</td></tr>
<tr><td>42</td><td>Nov 27, 1941</td><td>1338</td><td>I-16</td><td>VVS Southern Front</td><td>Rostov</td></tr>
<tr><td>43</td><td>Nov 29, 1941</td><td>0728</td><td>I-16</td><td>VVS Southern Front</td><td>Rostov</td></tr>
<tr><td>44</td><td>Dec 1, 1941</td><td>1503</td><td>DB-3</td><td>DBA</td><td>Taganrog</td></tr>
<tr><td>45</td><td rowspan="2">Dec 2, 1941</td><td>0815</td><td>I-61</td><td>VVS Southern Front</td><td rowspan="2">Taganrog</td></tr>
<tr><td>46</td><td>1210</td><td>I-16</td><td>VVS Southern Front</td></tr>
<tr><td>47</td><td rowspan="2">Dec 5, 1941</td><td>1008</td><td>I-16</td><td>VVS Southern Front</td><td rowspan="2">Taganrog</td></tr>
<tr><td>48</td><td>1009</td><td>I-61</td><td>VVS Southern Front</td></tr>
<tr><td>49</td><td>Dec 6, 1941</td><td>0831</td><td>I-16</td><td>VVS Southern Front</td><td>Taganrog</td></tr>
<tr><td>50</td><td>Dec 7,1941</td><td>1352</td><td>I-16</td><td>VVS Southern Front</td><td>Taganrog</td></tr>
</table>

51	Dec 8, 1941	0950	I-15	VVS Southern Front	Taganrog
52		0950	I-15	VVS Southern Front	
53		1310	I-16	VVS Southern Front	
54	Dec 9, 1941	1231	I-15	VVS Southern Front	Taganrog
55		1232	I-15	VVS Southern Front	
56		1236	I-15	VVS Southern Front	
57		1245	SB-2	VVS Southern Front	
58	Dec 11, 1941	0935	SB-2	VVS Southern Front	Taganrog
59		1334	I-26	VVS Southern Front	
60		1340	SB-2	VVS Southern Front	
61	Dec 22, 1941	1505	I-16	88 IAP	Taganrog
62		1510	I-16	88 IAP	
63	Feb 15, 1942	1404	Pe-2	VVS Southern Front	Belgorod
64		1548	I-61	VVS Southern Front	
65		1551	Il-2	VVS Southern Front	
66	Feb 18, 1942	0850	I-26	VVS Southern Front	Belgorod
67		0852	I-26	VVS Southern Front	
68	Feb 21, 1942	1232	I-16	VVS Southern Front	Belgorod
69	Feb 22, 1942	1535	V-11	VVS Southern Front	Belgorod
70		1537	V-11	VVS Southern Front	
71		1539	I-2	VVS Southern Front	
72		1542	U-2	VVS Southern Front	
73	Apr 25, 1942	1140	I-16	VVS Crimean Front	unspecified
74	Apr 29, 1942	1755	I-154	VVS Crimean Front	Kerch
75	Apr 30, 1942	1645	I-61	VVS Crimean Front	Kerch
76	May 1, 1942	0430	R-5	VVS Crimean Front	Kerch
77		0431	Su-2	VVS Crimean Front	
78		0434	Su-2	VVS Crimean Front	
79		0458	I-61	VVS Crimean Front	
80	May 2, 1942	0436	I-15	VVS Crimean Front	Kerch
81		0508	I-15	VVS Crimean Front	
82		0855	I-153	VVS Crimean Front	
83		01:05	MiG-3	VVS Crimean Front	
84		1810	I-16	VVS Crimean Front	
85	May 5, 1942	1113	MiG-1	VVS Crimean Front	N Kerch

A mechanic checks Fw. Beerenbrock's radio at Viazma, May 1942. It is a Bf 109F-2 as shown by the "C3" inscription (just visible at the bottom right) which characterizes the 96-octane fuel used by the DB 601 N engine of this version of the "Friedrich."

Leutnant Franz-Josef Beerenbrock

The Westphalian Franz-Josef Beerenbrock was born in Datteln, near Dortmund, on April 9, 1920. Through his mother, he came from a White Russian family. After completing his studies, he served in a Flak battalion in 1938, but a year later he started pilot training. His first posting was to IV./JG 51, and he joined the unit at Le Touquet in March 1941. However, he did not experience his real baptism of fire until *Barbarossa*. In this first days of combat in the East, missions were undertaken in the Brest-Litowsk–Mogilev sector. As *Katschmarek* (wingman) to Oblt. Karl-Gottfried Nordmann, *Staka* of 12. Staffel, Beerenbrock won his first two victories as early as June 24 as well as shooting up a number of tanks. The *Geschwader*, under Mölders, was tasked principally with covering Guderian's panzer force. The collaboration was exemplary, according to Guderian. The young Beerenbrock was actively involved in the mopping-up operation in the air. On July 30, he shot down a Pe-2 on the Bobruïsk airfield. At the beginning of July, the unit was based at Stara-Bychov, right on the enemy front lines. A week later, the unit reached Smolensk. Uffz. Beerenbrock accumulated victories in record time, his scoreboard already showing 25 victories by August 12, 1941. In the meantime, he had integrated the *Stabstaffel* of IV./JG 51 with Nordmann. This fighter *Gruppe* saw action over the Bryansk and Viazma sectors. The Knight's Cross was awarded to Franz-Josef on October 6 for his 42 successes.

But "General Winter" was to facilitate the great Soviet offensive that began on December 5 in front of Moscow. While Army Group Center retreated, Ofw. Beerenbrock won his 50th victory on December 6 from

Fw. Franz-Josef Beerenbrock photographed after the award of the German Cross in Gold on June 17, 1942. He also wears the Iron Cross 1st Class (July 18, 1941), the Frontflugspange (fighter clasp) and his airman's license on his jacket. Beerenbrock was awarded the Knight's Cross on October 6, 1941. There are comparatively few photographs of this understated ace.

These photos were taken at Dugino in early August 1942, when Franz-Josef had just broken the record of 101 victories held by Werner Mölders in JG 51. On August 1, in three sorties, Beerenbrock shot down nine aircraft: two MiG-3s and two Il-2s in the morning, one around noon, and three Il-2s, as well as a Pe-2 in the afternoon. He was awarded the Oak Leaves on August 3, 1942.

Beerenbrock's personal insignia painted on the fuselage of his 109: a large bullet being fired from a musket. The inscription "*Waidmannsheil!*" can be translated as "Good hunting!"

the airfield at Iermolino. Faced with the pressure of the Red Army, IV./JG 51 was employed in *Jabo*-type missions during the winter of 1941/2, when the weather allowed it, as temperatures plunged to 45°F–50°F below zero and immobilized most of the aircraft. In February, the *Jagdgruppe* was directed towards the Rjev sector in support of the German 9th Army. Beerenbrock shot down nine fighters in one week. Despite the end of the winter, air activity eased up in the spring. The ace claimed only 3 victories in April and 4 in May in the Viazma sector.

The fighting was more ferocious during the *Fall Blau* operation, the German summer offensive of 1942. The daily confrontations quickly raised Beerenbrock's score—the ace shot down nine aircraft on August 1 alone! He thus became the first pilot of JG 51 to surpass the record of 101 victories achieved by Mölders, whose name the *Geschwader* now bore. He added the Oak Leaves to his Knight's Cross on August 3 and was promoted to *Leutnant*.

After a long period of rest, he returned to the unit at the end of October as Staffelführer of 10./JG 51. Statistics show that many pilots were shot down after a long absence from the front. On November 9, 1942, Beerenbrock shot down three Pe-2s in the Zapadnodvinsk area; however, in the excitement of the fight, he did not see a LaGG-3 of the 249 IAP opening fire behind him and had to make a forced landing at the controls of Bf 109F-2 W.Nr. 6779 "White 12" behind enemy lines north of Welish. Soviet propaganda attributed this notable success to the ace Piotr Kozatchenko (27 victories). One of the greatest pilots of JG 51 thus fell into enemy hands.

Photographed during the fall of 1942, Bf 109F-2 "White 1" is probably the aircraft of the new *Staka* of 10./JG 51, Lt. Beerenbrock.

According to a rumor, the German pilot subsequently joined the pro-Soviet committee Freies Deutschland (National Committee for a Free Germany) while in captivity. It was even claimed that Beerenbrock shared his combat experience by training Soviet pilots. But the same claim was made about the JG 5 ace Rudolf Müller, who died in a POW camp. We know today that Fw 190s and Bf 109s marked with red stars and flown by "turned" German POWs are the stuff of myth. However, it is known that many prisoners of war signed a "confession" to avoid mistreatment and starvation. After seven years of captivity, Beerenbrock was able to return home in December 1949. The fact that he was quickly accepted into the Bundesluftwaffe at the height of the Cold War negated any suspicion that he was collaborating with the Soviet enemy. In total he had claimed 117 victories (112 confirmed) during 400 combat sorties. He died on December 13, 2004.

Beerenbock's victories

No	Date	Time	**Aircraft**	**Unit**	**Place**
1	Jun 24, 1941	0935	SB-2	13 BAD	Grudopole
2		0938	SB-2	13 BAD	
3	Jun 30, 1941	1315	R-10 (Il-2)	4 ChAP	Bobrouïsk
4	Jul 4, 1941	1845	SB-2		30km E of Syrtow
5	Jul 4, 1941	0635	DB-3		10km SE of Borrisov

6	Jul 6, 1941	1745	DB-3		Orcha sector
7		1750	DB-3		
8	Jul 9, 1941	0445	DB-3		Orcha sector
9		1125	DB-3		
10	Jul 10, 1941	1042	Pe-2	410 BAP	Orcha sector
11	Jul 11, 1941	0545	DB-3	410 BAP's 2nd platoon	Bobruysk sector
12	Jul 12, 1941	0920	DB-3		Bobruysk sector
13	Jul 13, 1941	0925	DB-3		Bobruysk sector
14	Jul 23, 1941	1305	Pe-2	410 or 411 BAP	Shatalovka sector
15		1820	Pe-2	410 or 411 BAP	Smolensk sector
16	Jul 24, 1941	0620	I-18 (MiG-1)		Smolensk sector
17		1210	Pe-2	410 BAP	
18	Jul 26, 1941	0428	R-3 (Il-2)		Smolensk sector
19	Jul 29, 1941	0428	I-16	32 IAP	Smolensk sector
20	Jul 31, 1941	1920	R-10		Smolensk sector
21	Aug 8, 1941	1215	R-3 (Il-2)		Velikie Luki sector
22	Aug 9, 1941	1216	Pe-2	47 SAD	Shatalovo sector
23		1415	I-16		nr Ielnia
24		1442	Pe-2		
25	Aug 12, 1941	1205	I-61 (MiG-3)		Bryansk sector
26		1215	I-16		
27	Aug 14, 1941	1900	I-18 (MiG-1)		Bryansk sector
28	Aug 15, 1941	1520	I-18 (MiG-1)		Bryansk sector
29	Aug 16, 1941	1908	I-18 (MiG-1)		Bryansk sector
30	Aug 19, 1941	1710	I-16		Bryansk sector
31	Aug 21, 1941	1655	Pe-2		Bryansk sector
32	Aug 25, 1941	1758	DB-3		SE of Porunovka
33		1802	DB-3		
34	Aug 26, 1941	1415	R-3 (Il-2)	4 ChAP	S of Chechinskaya
35		1420	R-3 (Il-2)	4 ChAP	
36	Aug 27, 1941	0906	I-18 (MiG-1)		SE of Novgorod
37		0909	I-18 (MiG-1)		
38	Aug 30, 1941	1503	I-18 (MiG-1)		10km SE of Chechinskaya
39		1505	I-18 (MiG-1)		8km SE of Chechinskaya
40		1509	I-18 (MiG-1)		5km SE of Chechinskaya
41	Sep 23, 1941	1602	SB-3		Shatalovka sector
42		1605	SB-3		

43	Oct 7, 1941	1245	Pe-2		Yukhnov sector
44	Oct 7, 1941	1330	Pe-2		Yukhnov sector
45	Oct 7, 1941	1635	I-18 (MiG-1)		Yukhnov sector
46	Oct 12, 1941	1425	Pe-2	46 BAP	Moscow sector
47	Dec 2, 1941	0915	I-61 (MiG-3)		Moscow sector
48	Dec 2, 1941	1120	Pe-2		Moscow sector
49	Dec 2, 1941	1123	Pe-2		Moscow sector
50	Dec 6, 1941	1355	I-16		Moscow sector
51	Dec 14, 1941	14h45	I-18 (MiG-1)		
52	Feb 23, 1942	1145	I-18 (MiG-1		Kalinin Front 30km E of Gargarin
53	Feb 23, 1942	1148	I-18 (MiG-1)		Kalinin Front 30km E of Gargarin
54	Feb 24, 1942	0920	I-18 (MiG-1)		30km E of Gargarin
55	Feb 26, 1942	1215	MiG-3	120 IAP	40km E of Gargarin
56	Mar 26, 1942	1158	MiG-3	VVS	Kalinin Front Dugino area
57	Mar 26, 1942	0755	MiG-1	VVS	Kalinin Front Dugino area
58	Mar 26, 1942	0759	MiG-1	VVS	Kalinin Front Dugino area
59	Mar 26, 1942	1630	MiG-1	VVS	Kalinin Front Dugino area
60	Apr 1, 1942	1055	MiG-3	VVS	Kalinin Front Viazma sector
61	Apr 7, 1942	0915	R-5	VVS	Kalinin Front Viazma sector
62	Apr 22, 1942	0640	MiG-3	VVS	Kalinin Front Viazma sector
63	May 27, 1941	1635	MiG-1		Viazma sector
64	May 28, 1941	0435	MiG-1		Viazma sector
65	May 28, 1941	0445	U-2		Viazma sector
66	May 28, 1941	1835	MiG-1		Viazma sector
67	June 1, 1942	0750	LaGG-3		Viazma sector
68	June 5, 1942	1820	Il-2		Viazma sector
69	June 11, 1942	1750	MiG-3		Viazma sector
70	June 16, 1942	1730	MiG-3		Viazma sector
71	June 25, 1942	0428	Yak-1		NW of Mochaisk
72	June 26, 1942	1800	MiG-3		Mamonovo sector
73	June 28, 1942	1510	MiG-3		Mamonovo sector
74	June 28, 1942	1950	Pe-2		Mamonovo sector
75	Jul 5, 1942	0405	Pe-2		Mamonovo sector
76	Jul 6, 1942	0555	Il-2		Mamonovo sector
77	Jul 6, 1942	0600	Il-2		Mamonovo sector
78	Jul 6, 1942	1939	I-16		Mamonovo sector
79	Jul 6, 1942	1945	I-16		Mamonovo sector

80	Jul 7, 1942	1740	LaGG-3		nr Belev
81	Jul 8, 1942	0540	LaGG-3		Viazma sector
82	Jul 9, 1942	1120	LaGG-3		Viazma sector
83		1655	LaGG-3		25km NE of Jizdra
84	Jul 10, 1942	0550	LaGG-3		Viazma sector
85		0555	LaGG-3		
86		1940	MiG-3		
87	Jul 11, 1942	0550	LaGG-3		S of Simnizy
88		1255	LaGG-3		Viazma sector
89		1930	Il-2		
90		1933	Il-2		
91	Jul 13, 1942	1600	MiG-3		W of Souchinitchi
92	Jul 28, 1942	1315	Pe-2		Viazma sector
93	Jul 31, 1942	1715	Il-2		16km NW of Rjev
94	Aug 1, 1942	1015	MiG-3		20km N of Rjev
95		1018	MiG-3		20km N of Rjev
96		1025	Il-2		15km N of Rjev
97		1028	Il-2		15km N of Rjev
98		1237	Il-2		20km W of Rjev
99		1625	Il-2		15km NW of Rjev
100		1627	Il-2		20km NW of Rjev
101		1630	Il-2		20km NE of Rjev
102		1635	Pe-2		Soubzov
103	Sep 30, 1942	1430	U-2		20km SE of Waldai
104		1445	MiG-3		80km NW of Waldai
105	Oct 2, 1942	1428	LaGG-3		5km SW of Krestzy
106	Oct 4, 1942	0855	LaGG-3		5km SE of Krestzy
107		0900	LaGG-3		2km N of Krestzy
108		1412	DB-3		25km SW of Bologiye
-	Nov 7, 1941	0742	MiG-3		nr Staraya Toropa
109	Nov 8, 1941	1445	MiG-3		15km NW of Toropa
110		1450	MiG-3		40km SW of Staraya Toropa
111		1450	MiG-3		
112	Nov 9, 1941	0742	Pe-2		
-		0742	Pe-2		SW of Staraya Toropa
-		0742	Pe-2		SW of Staraya Toropa

2
Day Fighter Aces: West

The Western Front, that area stretching from Denmark to the Pyrenees, can roughly be divided into two distinct timeframes: firstly, the *Westfeldzug* (campaign in the West) which encompassed the invasion of the Low Countries and France, and the subsequent battle of Britain, and, secondly, D-Day and its aftermath, including the disastrous Operation *Bodenplatte* which saw the Luftwaffe taken to the edge of annihilation.

In this chapter we consider seven German aviators, who achieved their victories mainly in the West. Leading the charge is the prodigious Joachim Müncheberg with 135 victories, followed by Adolf Galland with 104. Galland would likely have achieved a far higher total had he not been pulled off operations to become Inspector of Fighters. Josef Wurmheller, with 102 victories, had an unusually "long" career—from September 1, 1939, to June 22, 1944, when he was killed in action. Karl Willius achieved 50 victories and Wilhelm Balthasar 40. We've also included Franz von Werra (19 kills) for his brief and colorful career. Finally, we look at a different type of ace, Frank Liesendahl, who claimed 11 ships sunk.

Major Wilhelm Balthasar

Born on February 2, 1914, in Fulda, Wilhelm Balthasar did not know his father, Hptm. August Balthasar, who was killed at Neuve-Chapelle on October 14, 1914, in the Great War. Enlisting in the army in 1933, he left the artillery two years later to join the Luftwaffe despite his short-sightedness. In late 1936, he reached Spain, initially flying with the K/88 bombing group on Heinkel 70s or Junkers 52s; there he and his observer were credited with a victory over an I-16 on January 20, 1937. On March 15, he was transferred to the Versuchsjagdgruppe 88 (VJ/88), an experimental fighter group flying the He 112, but in September he was moved to 1. J/88 where he shot down a second I-16 at the controls of a Bf 109C. On February 7, 1938, his *Staffel* sortied to attack Republican positions near Teruel, but encountered a formation of SB-2s near Valencia. Balthasar made his mark by shooting down four of these bombers as well as an escort fighter. Returning to Germany in March

Photographed on March 7, 1939, on their return from an expeditionary flight to Africa, from left: Oblt. Wilhelm Balthasar, Uffz. Karl Anhäuser (probably the expedition's mechanic), and Oblt. Rolf Kaldrack, a future Bf 110 Knight's Cross holder, killed in 1942.

Oblt. Balthasar, *Staka* of 1./JG 1, received the Iron Cross 2nd Class on September 23, 1939 at Dummersee.

1938, he was acknowledged as the longest-serving Condor Legion pilot in Spain. Flying in reconnaissance, then in ground support and finally as a fighter, he made no less than 465 combat flights. Always adventurous, Balthasar then took part in an expeditionary flight to Africa: 40,000 kilometers from January 16 to March 7, 1939. Having become *Staffelkapitän* of 1./JG 1 in 1939, he was not involved in the campaign against Poland, but made up for it during the May/June 1940 campaign in the West.

On Saturday May 11, during a *Freie Jagd* over the Belgian border, he attacked a formation of Gloster Gladiators of the Belgian Aéronautique Militaire (1/I/2 AE. Mi.) One of his projectiles exploded in the fuselage of the aircraft of 1st Sgt Denys Rollin who was able to parachute out. Two other biplanes fell to his fire. In the evening, Balthasar brought down an M.S.406. Following a string of victories over the next few days, he was quickly recognized as a mentor by the young guard of 1./JG 1: Ludwig Franzisket, Gerhard Homuth, and Wolfgang Redlich, all future Knight's Cross holders. On May 23, on a mission to escort *Zerstörer* heavy fighters, Hptm. Balthasar downed three Hurricanes over the Calais–Dunkirk sector. Three days later, he claimed two Spitfires over Calais. After the fall of Dunkirk, the RAF was almost completely absent from the skies over France and the Luftwaffe was able to deliver the finishing blow to the Armée de l'Air. On June 5, the ace claimed two LeO 451s, two M.S.406s, and a Potez 63 over the course of two sorties. With 23 victories in the air and 13 planes destroyed on the ground, he was the leading Luftwaffe fighter pilot of the *Westfeldzug* (campaign in the West) and was the second fighter pilot behind Werner Mölders to be awarded the Knight's Cross (June 14, 1940).

After a short rest, the hero of the campaign was engaged in the battle of Britain in mid-July. However, he left 1./JG 1 because he was assigned for a while to the fighter training school in Werneuchen before taking command of III./JG 3 at the beginning of September, when the Luftwaffe intensified its raids on RAF airfields.

The tail of Bf 109E-4 W.Nr. 1559 photographed a few days later, when its pilot's tally had risen to 20 aerial victories (arrows pointing up) and 11 aircraft destroyed on the ground (arrows pointing down).

Nummer 42 12. Oktober 1940

49. Jahrgang Preis 20 Pfennig

Berliner Illustrirte Zeitung

Neuer Roman von Maria v. Kirchbach

Unablässig gegen England

The cover of the *Berliner Illustrirte Zeitung*, October 12, 1940: Wilhelm Balthasar climbing out of his "Emil" during the battle of Britain.

Flying out of Desvres on September 4, he was in combat with Spitfires over Canterbury but took hits from a No. 222 Squadron machine and was wounded in the leg. However, on September 23, while still walking with a cane, he took part in a mission over the south of England during which he sent two Spitfires crashing into the sea, firing only 88 rounds of ammunition. He had three more successes before being withdrawn from the Channel front. Given the after-effects of his battle on the 4th, Balthasar had to undergo surgery and remained in hospital for several weeks.

On February 16, 1941, the ace was appointed to command JG 2. On May 7, he shot down a Spitfire from No. 54 Squadron off the coast of Dover and, two days later, a Blenheim operating at low altitude in the Baie de Seine (Bay of the Seine or south of the Isle of Wight).

On June 22, 1941, RAF Circus No. 18 targeted Hazebrouck, near Dunkirk. The *Kommodore* was credited with two Blenheims, although there is no archive record of either of these "losses." At Ligescourt in northern France, Gerhard Schöpfel, then *Kommandeur* of III./JG 26 recalled meeting the new *Kommodore* during this period;

In June 1941 my *Gruppe* was reinforced with the arrival on our airfield at Ligescourt of a *Gruppe* from JG 2 "Richthofen." Shortly thereafter, their *Kommodore*, Hptm. Balthasar flew in and I had the opportunity to talk with him. He was a very nice fellow and the fact that we had the same rank meant that we indulged in a frank exchange of views. His reputation as a Condor Legion ace and then as the leading pilot of the 1940 campaign had preceded him. However, I did not know then that his career had been interrupted following an injury. He longed to relaunch his ascension to the pantheon of

Now *Kommodore* of JG 2, Hptm. Balthasar posed for a snapshot in the cabin of a Bf 109E-4 still equipped with the old type of canopy, around February/March 1941.

Balthasar and his preferred wingman, Oblt. Erich Leie from his *Stabsschwarm*, seen here in early 1941 in front of the former's Bf 109E-7/N prior to the arrival of the first "Friedrichs" in JG 2.

the great fighter aces in the German fighter arm. He didn't fail to congratulate me on the impressive track record of my *Gruppe*. I also learned that he had never known his father and his wife would soon give birth. I've often reflected since on the destinies of families that recur across generations. A scramble was triggered in the early evening (June 23, 1941) and Balthasar suggested I combine the two *Gruppen*—which I wasn't too keen on—my *Schwarm* leading the formation, followed by his. We rushed out to our aircraft, and it wasn't long before we came across a group of enemy twin-engined bombers. As I was leading the formation, I threw myself on the first enemy machine and quickly downed it. Balthasar took the second in his sights and finished him off. I then saw him perform a loop that took him underneath the third. Pulling up, he unleashed several bursts which accounted for that one in short order. When we landed back at the airfield, I could only congratulate him on his flying skill and marksmanship.

Balthasar's "brand-new" yellow-nosed Bf 109F-2, most probably only just received at JG 2. His rudder scoreboard shows 31 victories, dating the picture to around late May or early June 1941.

Once again, these two Blenheim claims on June 23 cannot be identified with certainty from British records. On June 27, 1941, JG 2 intercepted Circus No. 25 launched towards Lille. Balthasar claimed the destruction of a Spitfire and a Blenheim. No. 19 Squadron lost two aircraft and the 74th lost three, including that of its CO, Sqn Ldr John Mungo-Park. These were Balthasar's 39th and 40th victories in World War II; he was subsequently awarded the Knight's Cross with Oak Leaves, becoming the 17th member of the Wehrmacht to be so honored.

On July 3, 1941, a few days after he was able to take a short leave of absence to finally meet his newborn son, the ace crashed and was killed in the hamlet of Saint-Martin (on the road from Saint-Omer to Aire sur la Lys). He was either shot down by Sqn Ldr Michael Lister-Robinson (No. 609 Squadron), or was the victim of a high-g maneuver that tore off the wings of his new Bf 109 "Friedrich." In accordance with his wishes, the officer—posthumously promoted to *Major*—was buried in the Great War military cemetery at Illies alongside his father.

Balthasar's victories

No	Date	Time	Aircraft	Unit	Place
SPAIN					
1	Jan 20, 1937		I-16		Madrid area
2	Jan 20, 1938		I-16		Teruel area
3	Feb 7, 1938		SB-2		Valencia area
4			SB-2		
5			SB-2		
6			SB-2		
7			I-16		
World War II					
1	May 11, 1940	0655	Gladiator	Aé Mi. 1/I/2 (Belgian)	Albert Canal
2		0666	Gladiator		
3		0658	Gladiator		
4		1951	M.S.406		E of Maastricht
5	May 13, 1940	0615	Hurricane		Jodoigne

6	May 17, 1940	1355	Curtiss H-75		Compiègne
7	May 19, 1940	1350	Lysander	16 Sqn	Amiens
8	May 23, 1940	1410	Hurricane		Douai
8		1425	Hurricane		
10		1440	Hurricane		
11	May 26, 1940	1003	Spitfire	19 Sqn	Calais
12		1003	Spitfire	19 Sqn	
13	Jun 5, 1940	1040	LeO 451		Montdidier
14		1048	Po 63		Nesle
15		1050	LeO 451		Nesle
16		2120	M.S.406		Roye
17		2130	M.S.406		
18	Jun 6, 1940	1640	M.S.406	GB II/2	Roye
19		1650	LeO 451	GB II/2	
20		1700	LeO 451	GB II/2	
21		1705	LeO 451	GB II/2	Sézanne
22	Jun 13, 1940	1750	Po 63	GAR I/14	Provins
23		1820			
24	Sep 4, 1940	1100	Spitfire	66 Sqn	SE of London
25	Sep 23, 1940		Spitfire		S of Chatham
26			Spitfire		N of Cap Gris-Nez
27	Sep 27, 1940	1425	Spitfire		Kent
28	Oct 29, 1940	1640	Spitfire		
29		1645	Spitfire		
30	May 17, 1941	1855	Spitfire II	54 Sqn	off Dover
31	May 19, 1941	2020	Blenheim		S of Isle of Wight
32	Jun 22, 1941	1600	Blenheim		Saint-Omer/Gravelines
33		1602	Blenheim		
34	Jun 23, 1941	2030	Blenheim		Mardyck
35		2033	Blenheim		N of Dunkirk
36	Jun 24, 1941	2050	Spitfire	603 or 611 Sqn	Gravelines/Ramsgate
37	Jun 25, 1941	1300	Spitfire		Hazebrouck/Gravelines
38		1645	Spitfire		Saint-Omer/Boulogne
39	Jun 27, 1941	2203	Spitfire	19 or 74 Sqn	Lille/Gravelines
40		2207	Blenheim		Lille/Gravelines

Oberleutnant Karl Willius

Born on November 5, 1919 in Mainz, Karl Willius joined the Luftwaffe in 1939 and was transferred in May 1940 to 8./JG 51. He did not fight in the *Westfeldzug* but made up for it in the battle of Britain returning the first of four victories on August 18. In May 1941 he went east with III./JG 51, having been awarded the Front Flying Clasp (Frontflugspange) in Gold. Following the opening of *Barbarossa*, Willius quickly added 12 *Luftsiegen* to his score. He then seems to have volunteered to return to fight in the West. On August 1, 1941, he was transferred to 2./JG 26 on the Channel front. The subsequent award of the Ehrenpokal (Honor Goblet) testified to his competence in the air as a combat pilot. Again, fighting against the RAF, he added 12 further *Luftsiegen* to his score and was awarded the German Cross in Gold, usual a precurser to the Knight's Cross. At the end of 1942, having fought over Dieppe during the disastrous Canadian landings on August 19, 1942, "Charly" Willius left to serve as an instructor before returning to 2./JG 26 in April 1943. At that time, the unit was temporarily reassigned in the East (an exchange with III./JG 54 returned to the Channel) and Willius was able to add nine more Soviet aircraft to his scoreboard.

Seen here in mid-September 1940, at Saint-Omer airfield, Uffz. Karl Willius of 8./JG 51, looks at his three victory bars, all of which were won against RAF fighters. His machine was Bf 109E-4 W.Nr. 1989.

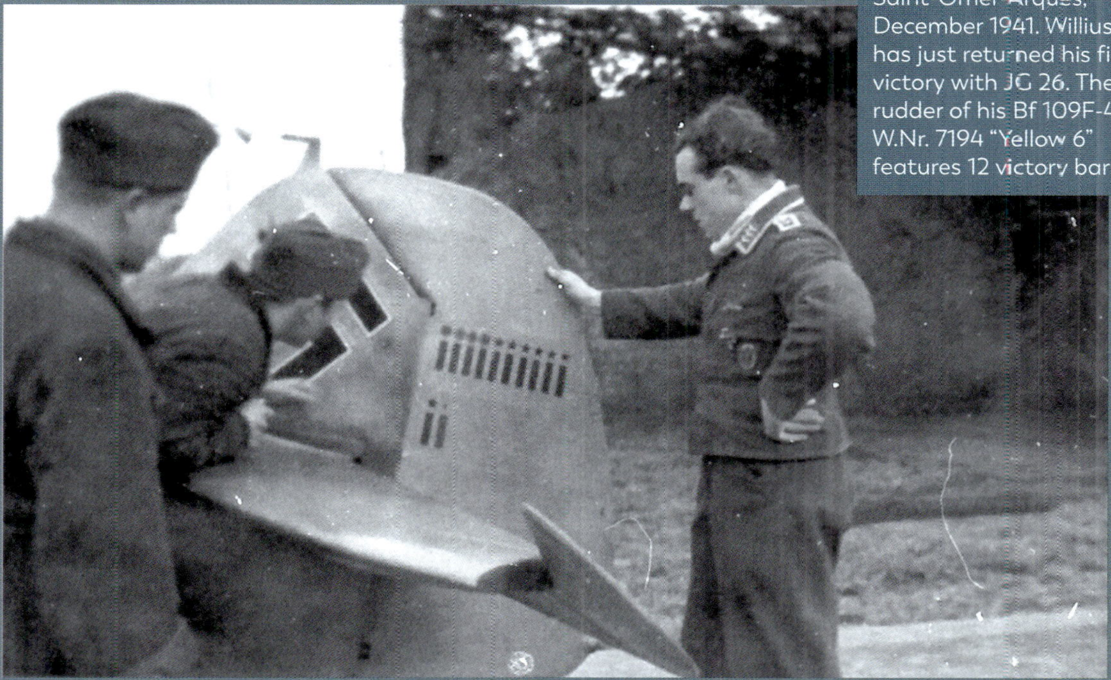

Saint-Omer-Arques, December 1941. Willius has just returned his first victory with JG 26. The rudder of his Bf 109F-4 W.Nr. 7194 "Yellow 6" features 12 victory bars.

Fw. "Charly" Willius standing on the wing of his Fw 190 "Yellow 5" in August 1942. Note the flags of the nations of his opponents under the cockpit sil . The first row of victories on his rudder are those credited while with JG 51—four RAF and seven Soviet machines—while the lower row represents his successes achieved with JG 26.

These victories earned him a promotion to *Leutnant*. Once back in the West, he was appointed *Staffelführer* of 2./JG 26, a role he would have carried out with competence. Hospitalized for a time in Belgium due to illness, he met a Belgian nurse from Louvain (Leuven) whom he married. A daughter was born shortly afterwards. On February 4, 1944, Willius achieved his 40th victory. On April 8, I./JG 26 was scrambled and directed over the Netherlands to engage a large bomber formation. Kapitän Willius downed a B-24 but fell victim to the escort fighters and his Fw 190 came down in the Zuiderzee (Netherlands). The Knight's Cross was awarded posthumously along with promotion to the rank of *Oberleutnant*. He had returned 50 victories, of which 48 were confirmed or *anerkannte Abschüsse*. On October 23, 1967, during operations to drain the Zuiderzee to reclaim land from the sea, an Fw 190 was recovered with the body of "Charly" Willius who, it was otherwise believed, had been buried for more than 20 years in a nearby military cemetery.

I./JG 26 Fw 190A-5 flown by Fw. Willius seen at Dno in early April 1943 marked with 23 victory bars. This type of victory scoreboard was rare on an Fw 190 in the East.

"Charly" Willius with his Belgian wife in the park of Florennes Castle in early 1944.

Willius's victories

No	Date	Time	Aircraft	Unit	Place
1	Aug 18, 1940		Spitfire		nr Ramsgate
2	Aug 31, 1940		Hurricane		
3	Sep 15, 1940		Spitfire		
4	Sep 30, 1940		Spitfire		
5	Jun 22, 1941		SB-2		
6	Jun 25, 1941		SB-2		
7	Jun 30, 1941		TB-3		
8			TB-3		
9	Jul 1, 1941		SB-2		
10	Jul 13, 1941		DB-3		
11			DB-3		
12	Aug 1941		unidentified		
13	Dec 8, 1941		Spitfire		nr Boulogne
14	Apr 10, 1942		Spitfire	313 Sqn	nr Calais
15	Apr 12, 1942		Spitfire	41 Sqn	S of Bourbourg
16	Apr 24, 1942		Spitfire	72 or 124 Sqn	nr Calais

17	Apr 27, 1942		Spitfire	457 or 485 Sqn	nr Dunkirk
18	May 17, 1942		Spitfire	64 or 122 Sqn	off Calais
19	May 23, 1942		Spitfire	350 Sqn	N of Calais
20	Jun 8, 1942		Spitfire		Arques area
21	Aug 18, 1942		Spitfire	602 Sqn	Cape Gris-Nez
22	Aug 19, 1942		Spitfire		off Dieppe
23	Dec 11, 1942		Defiant	277 Sqn	nr Dungeness
24	Dec 12, 1942		Spitfire	350 Sqn	off Wimereux
25	Apr 11, 1943		Lagg-4		
26	May 13, 1943		Pe-2		
27			Pe-2		
28			Pe-2		
29			MiG-3		
30	May 27, 1943		LaGG-3		
31	May 28, 1943		LaGG-3		
32	Jun 2, 1943		LaGG-3		
33			LaGG-3		
34	July 30, 1943		"Boston" (B-26)	386th BG	nr Antwerp
35	Aug 18, 1943		Spitfire		nr Ipswich
-	Sep 4, 1943		Spitfire	131 Sqn	nr Dunkirk
36	Dec 1, 1943		B-17		nr Koblenz
37	Dec 30, 1943		B-17	100th BG	Soissons
38	Jan 11, 1944		B-17	306th BG	Deventer
39	Jan 30, 1944		P-38		nr Coesfeld
40	Feb 4, 1944		B-17		nr Cousolre
41	Feb 6, 1944		B-17	96th BG	Melun
42	Feb 24, 1944		B-24		Giessen
43	Feb 25, 1944		B-26	387th BG	off Zeebrugge
44			B-26	387th BG	
45	Mar 2, 1944		B-17		Wiesbaden
46	Mar 6, 1944		B-17		N of Koblenz
47	Mar 15, 1944		B-24	392nd BG	E of Norwich
-	Mar 16, 1944		B-17		
48	Mar 23, 1944		B-17	385th BG	Tilburg
49	Mar 27, 1944		P-47	359th FG	S of Dreux
50	Apr 8, 1944		B-24	44th BG	Zwolle

Joachim Müncheberg was well known for his performances as a decathlete before the war.

Major Joachim Müncheberg

On November 7, 1939, JG 26 returned its first victory of World War II, the handiwork of a new III./JG 26 pilot. Shot down by Lt. Joachim Müncheberg, Blenheim L1325 of No, 57 Squadron crashed into the Rhine. Müncheberg, born on December 18, 1918, in the village of Fridrichsdorf in Pomerania, was known as a decathlon athlete before the war. A former member of I./JG 234, he made a brief transition to 10.(N)/JG 26 under Oblt. Johannes Steinhoff, then joined the staff flight of the new III./JG 26. He flew with JG 26 during May/June 1940 and was credited with eight aircraft during the offensive in the West. Over England, Müncheberg flew as wingman to the new *Kommodore* of JG 26, Obstlt. Adolf Galland, claiming his 10th victory against a Hurricane of No. 257 Squadron on July 28. The following

"Jochen" photographed in June 1940 in his Bf 109E, "chevron"-decorated with the insignia of the Stab III./JG 26: the number 13 in a four-leaf clover.

In February 1941, 7./JG 26 began operations over Malta from the Sicilian airfield of Gela. This partial view of Bf 109E-7/N "White 1" W.Nr. 5961 belonging to Oblt. Müncheberg reveals the ace's score on his arrival on the island: 23 victories.

Müncheberg in his new Messerschmitt "White 12" in Sicily, early May 1941. The antenna mast carries the pennant of the *Staffelkapitän*. Note the presence of a gun camera in the wing leading edge beside the blast tube of the 20mm machine gun.

Bf 109E-7/N W.Nr. 3826 displaying a score of 41 victories achieved by Müncheberg in the West. The last represents a Hurricane of No. 261 Squadron shot down on May 1, 1942.

month, he returned a further five victories. In the meantime, he was promoted to *Oberleutnant* and left the *Stab* to take over as *Staffelkapitän* of 7./JG 26 on August 22. On September 14, he obtained his 20th victory, which earned him the Knight's Cross.

In January 1941, 12 7./JG 26 Bf 109s departed the Belgian airfield of Wevelgem to reinforce X. Fliegerkorps in the Mediterranean. From Gela, Sicily, the *Staffel* flew 400 sorties over Malta and returned some 42 victories in three months without a single loss. Müncheberg alone shot down 20 aircraft; a biplane Avia BH.33E and a Breguet XIX destroyed on April 6 during the attack on Yugoslavia and a Short Sunderland seaplane machine-gunned in the bay of Kalafrana on April 27, were not, however, certified. On May 7, the so-called "Maltese Eagle" was decorated with the Oak Leaves and the very rare gold medal for Italian bravery, which was only ever awarded to two foreigners (the second being Hans-Joachim Marseille).

The ace returns from a mission, his face still marked by the effort. Müncheberg had the reputation of fighting with a single wingman or engaging alone.

On June 1, 7./JG 26, with only six Bf 109E-7s, moved to Gazala, Libya, to reinforce I./JG 27. The *Kapitän* was to win successive victories: three Hurricanes and two RAF and SAAF P-40s during the summer of 1941. At the end of August 7, Staffel was withdrawn from the African theater. As soon as "Jochen" Müncheberg returned to the Western Front, he recorded his 50th *Abschuss* on August 28. On September 19, he was promoted to *Hauptmann* and *Kommandeur* of II./JG 26 based at Moorsele, Belgium. Now at the controls of an Fw 190A-1, the aviator ended 1941 with a total of 62 claims. Between March 13 and April 30, he added 13 more successes to his victory scoreboard. On July 21, 1942, Müncheberg was sent to the Eastern Front, first as a temporary replacment for Obstlt. Karl-Gottfried Nordmann, then as his deputy. Facing the Soviet Air Force, he won 33 victories in four weeks in the Rjev–Soubzov sector where Army Group Center was operating. After his 100th *Abschuss* on September 5, he became the 13th Luftwaffe aviator to pin the Swords onto the ribbon of his Knight's

Post-sortie debrief. In Drucat, in the spring of 1942, the *Kommandeur* of II/JG 26 describes his last dogfight to "Wutz" Galland (right), the younger brother of the General der Jagdflieger. In the center is Oblt. Theodor Lindemann.

On March 27, 1942, a mechanic paints the 64th and 65th victory bars on the rudder of Fw 190A-2 W.Nr. 20209 flown by Hptm. Müncheberg. Three days earlier, the ace shot down two Spitfires of No. 412 Squadron RCAF near Cambron (Somme).

Maintenance work on Fw 190A-3 W.Nr. 257 flown by the *Gruppenkommandeur* in Drucat, early May 1942.

Rare view of Müncheberg during his training period at JG 51 during the summer 1942. Note the panel of III./JG 51 “Mölders” in the background.

Possibly the last photo of Müncheberg, by now *Kommodore* of JG 77, probably taken in March 1943 on the field at La Fauconnerie. He is seen inspecting his new Bf 109G-6 Trop.

Cross. His "training" completed in the Stab/JG 51, Major Müncheberg took over at the head of Jagdgeschwader 77 on October 1, 1942. His new *Geschwader* had to cover the German–Italian columns retreating into the Tunisian bridgehead after the failure of El Alamein. The *Geschwaderstab*, equipped with brand-new Bf 109G-2 Trop fighters, had to wait until November 5, 1942, to reach North Africa via Bari and Athens-Eleusis. Four days later, Kommodore Müncheberg returned his first two African victories by downing two Spitfires. However, his unit had to move constantly—Gambut, Benghazi, El Magrum and finally the Arco Philaenorum—following the German retreat. Always at the forefront of the fighting, Müncheberg was credited with a No. 1 SAAF Squadron aircraft on November 27 and a P-40 of the 66th FS/57th FG on December 10. During this last fight, the engine of his Bf 109G-2 W.Nr. 10725 was hit by the fire of Flt Lt Robert R. Smith, a Spitfire pilot of No. 112 Squadron. The JG 77 "boss" had to perform a belly-landing near the Arco Philaenorum (on the border between Cyrenaica and Tripolitania). Alongside his pilots, the *Kommodore* flew daily against large formations of Allied aircraft. On January 22, 1943, two aircraft of No. 3 RAAF Squadron were shot down by Müncheberg, who was then granted a three-week leave of absence. Meanwhile, Feldmarschall Rommel evacuated Tripoli and withdrew to the Mareth Line. On March 23, 1943, at 0930, Major Müncheberg and his wingman and comrade, Lt. Gerhard Strasen, took off from the Tunisian airfield at La Fauconnerie on a free-hunt sortie south of Gabès. Twenty minutes later, the *Rotte* intercepted a formation of 52nd FG Spitfires near Maknassy. Müncheberg, flying his 500th combat sortie, immediately attacked Captain Theodore Sweetland's aircraft. The Spitfire exploded in mid-air, but the German ace was unable to avoid the debris which struck his machine at high speed, causing a wing to buckle and break away. The Bf 109G-6 Trop W.Nr. 16381 went out of control and crashed near the Gabès–Gafsa road. The "Maltese Eagle" was buried a few days later in the cemetery of El-Aouina, in Tunis. He had returned 135 victories over all fronts.

A recipient of the Swords for his 135 victories won on all fronts, but primarily against the aircraft of the Western Allies, "Jochen" Müncheberg had earned the respect of his men and his superiors, who appreciated his leadership qualities.

Müncheberg's victories

No	Date	Time	Aircraft	Unit	Place
1	Nov 7, 1939	1343	Blenheim L1325	57 Sqn	SE Opladen
2	May 11, 1943	1745	Curtiss H-75A	GC I/4	NNE Antwerp
3	May 14, 1943	1845	Hurricane	504 Sqn	E of Ath
4	May 15, 1943	1300	Hurricane L1645	3 Sqn	Overijse
5	May 29, 1943	1810	Spitfire	64, 229, or 610 Sqn	W of Dunkirk
6	May 31, 1943	1535	Lysander	2 Sqn	In sea off De Panne
7	May 31, 1943	1540	Hurricane	213 or 264 Sqn	nr Dunkirk
8	May 31, 1943	1545	Hurricane	213 or 264 Sqn	nr Dunkirk
9	May 31, 1943	2030	Spitfire	609 Sqn	Dunkirk/Dover
10	Jul 28, 1940	1515	Hurricane	257 Sqn	15km NE of Dover
11	Aug 8, 1940	1255	Spitfire	65 Sqn	NE of Margate
12	Aug 8, 1940	1329	Hurricane	32 or 615 Sqn	Folkestone/Dover
13	Aug 8, 1940	1601	Spitfire	64 Sqn	SE of Dover
14	Aug 8, 1940	1322	Hurricane	151 Sqn	Ashford
15	Aug 8, 1940	1000	Hurricane	56 Sqn	NW of Braintree
16	Sep 1, 1940	1452	Hurricane	79 or 85 Sqn	W of Goodhurst
17	Sep 6, 1940	1028	Hurricane	303 (Polish) Sqn	Dungeness
18	Sep 7, 1940	1845	Spitfire	603 Sqn	SE of London
19	Sep 11, 1940	1925	Spitfire	66 or 92 Sqn	E of Ashford
20	Sep 14, 1940	1705	Spitfire	222 Sqn	S of Maidstone
21	Oct 17, 1940	1455	Bloch 151		Faversham
22	Oct 25, 1940	1440	Spitfire	2 Sqn	Marden
23	Nov 14, 1940	1532	Spitfire	66 or 74 Sqn	SE of Dover
24	Feb 12, 1941	1641	Hurricane	261 Sqn	S of Is-Siġġiewi
25	Feb 16, 1941	1038	Hurricane	261 Sqn	Venezia/Malta (one only damaged)
26	Feb 16, 1941	1045	Hurricane	261 Sqn	Venezia/Malta (one only damaged)
27	Feb 25, 1941	1645	Hurricane	261 Sqn	E of San Pawl il-Baħar
28	Feb 26, 1941	1406	Hurricane	261 Sqn	Malta/Krendi
29	Feb 26, 1941	1410	Hurricane	261 Sqn	Malta/Krendi
30	Mar 2, 1941	1045	Fulmar 806	RNAS Sqn	2 km W of Marsaxlokk
31	Mar 5, 1941	1732	Hurricane	261 Sqn	S of Hal Far
32	Mar 15, 1941	0750	Wellington W5644	Reserve Flt	10km NE of Gozo
33	Mar 28, 1941	1732	Hurricane	261 Sqn	10km S of Gozo
34	Apr 6, 1941	1205	Avia BH 33	Esk 81	NE of Podgorica
-	Apr 6, 1941		Avia BH-33E	Esk 81 Breguet XIX 3rd Flying School	Podgorica

35	Apr 11, 1941	1131	Hurricane	261 Sqn	SE of Malta
36		1153	Hurricane	261 Sqn	San Pawl il-Baħar
37	Apr 23, 1941	1807	Hurricane	261 Sqn	SE of Hal Far
-	Apr 27, 1941		Sunderland L5807	228 Sqn	Kalafrana
38	Apr 29, 1941	1847	Hurricane	261 Sqn	San Pawl il-Baħar
39	May 1, 1941	0753	Hurricane	261 Sqn	La Valette/Luqa
40		0753	Hurricane	261 Sqn	
41		1715	Hurricane	261 Sqn	Luqa
42	May 6, 1941	1222	Hurricane	261 Sqn	NE of San Pawl il-Baħar
43		1226	Hurricane	261 Sqn	nr Hal Far
-	May 25, 1941		2 x Hurricanes	249 Sqn	Ta'Quali
44	Jun 20, 1941	0755	Hurricane	1 or 2 (SAAF) Sqn	20km E of Buqbuq
45	Jun 24, 1941	0755	Hurricane	6 Sqn	Lauyet Ungheila
46	Jul 15, 1941	1840	Hurricane	73 or 229 Sqn	
47	Jul 29, 1941	1748	P-40	2 (RAAF) Sqn	SE of Ghar el Melh
48		1752	P-40	2 (RAAF) Sqn	50km E of Bardia
49	Aug 26, 1941	1930	Spitfire	611 Sqn	2km N of Gravelines
50	Aug 29, 1941	0840	Spitfire		10km NE of Dunkirk
51	Sep 4, 1941	1726	Spitfire		Vollezele
52		1729	Spitfire		Zegerscappel
53	Sep 7, 1941	1722	Spitfire V	71 Sqn	NE of Montreuil
54	Sep 16, 1941	1722	Spitfire	306 or 315 (Polish) Sqn	E of Boulogne
55	Sep 18, 1941	1606	Hurricane II	607 Sqn	Yvetot
56		1615	Spitfire	452 (RAAF) Sqn	Sainte-Hélène
57	Oct 13, 1941	1433	Spitfire V		
58	Nov 8, 1941	1307	Spitfire V	412 (RCAF) Sqn	Loon-Plage
59		1315	Spitfire V	412 (RCAF) Sqn	NNE of Dunkirk
-	Dec 8, 1941		Spitfire V	412 (RCAF) Sqn	nr Dunkirk
60		1417	Spitfire V		E of Boulogne
61	Dec 16, 1941	10601	Spitfire V	411 (RCAF) Sqn	N of Dunkirk
62		1604	Spitfire V	411 (RCAF) Sqn	N of Gravelines
63	Mar 13, 1942	1617	Spitfire	124 Sqn	Wierre/Effroy
64	Mar 24, 1942	1630	Spitfire	412 (RCAF) Sqn	NE Rue/Cambron
65		1635	Spitfire	412 (RCAF) Sqn	
66	Apr 4, 1942	1146	Spitfire		off Calais
67	Apr 10, 1942	1750	Spitfire		NE Etaples

68	Apr 25, 1942	1640	Spitfire		SE Crécy
69		1643	Spitfire		SE Rue
70	Apr 26, 1942	1805	Spitfire	485 (RNZAF) Sqn	ENE of Calais
71		1806	Spitfire	485 (RNZAF) Sqn	E of Cape Gris Nez
72	Apr 27, 1942	1447	Spitfire	Tangmere Wing or 340 (French) Sqn	NE of Dunkirk
73		1606	Spitfire	303 Sqn	N of Mardyck
74	Apr 29, 1942	1604	Spitfire	Northolt Wing or 317 (Polish) Sqn	Le Touquet
75	Apr 30, 1942	1936	Spitfire	222 Sqn	Somme estuary
76	May 1, 1942	1931	Spitfire	122 or 222 Sqn	SE of Calais
-		1940	Spitfire		5km E of Calais
77	May 6, 1942	1853	Spitfire	303 (Polish) Sqn	N of Cape Gris-Nez
-	May 9, 1942	1343	Spitfire	118 or 501 Sqn	15km S of Gravelines
-		1344	Spitfire	118 or 501 Sqn	
-	May 17, 1942	1735	Spitfire		Guînes/Saint-Omer
78	May 31, 1942	1937	Spitfire	485 (RNZAF) Sqn	S of Crécy Forest
79		1941	Spitfire	302 Sqn	Quend/Plage-les-Pins
80	Jun 2, 1941	1101	Spitfire	403 (RCAF) Sqn	SE Abbeville
81		1107	Spitfire	403 (RCAF) Sqn	15km W of Etaples
82	Jun 2, 1941	1544	Spitfire	118 or 501 Sqn	S Ardres E of Boulogne
83		1547	Spitfire	118 or 501 Sqn	
84	Aug 3, 1942	1032	Pe-2		nr Rjev
85		1036	Pe-2		
86	Aug 4, 1942	1038	Il-2		6km ENE of Soubzov
87	Aug 5, 1942	1848	LaGG-3		10km SE of Rogatschev
88	Aug 9, 1942	1430	MiG-3		10km SE of Soubzov
89	Aug 10, 1942	1840	Yak-1		15km N of Rjev
90	Aug 22, 1942	1025	Il-2		15km SSE of Soubzov
91	Aug 24, 1942	0620	Il-2		nr Rjev
92		0621	Il-2		
93	Aug 25, 1942	1711	Il-2		30km NNW of Rjev
94	Sep 2, 1942	0823	LaGG-3		SW of Karmanovo
95		1052	Il-2		nr Gagarine
96		1053	Il-2		
97		1055	Il-2		
98	Sep 3, 1942	1432	Il-2		nr Konaja
99	Sep 4, 1942	1735	Pe-2		S of Soubzov

100	Sep 5, 1942	1753	Airacobra		Koubinka
101		1755	Airacobra		15km ENE of Mojaïsk
102	Sep 9, 1942	1708	Il-2		5km SE de Rjev
103		1712	Il-2		15km WSW of Soubzov
104	Sep 10, 1942	0709	Pe-2		10km SSE of Soubzov
105		0713	Il-2		NW of Soubzov
106		1035	LaGG-3		8km ESE of Rjev
107	Sep 13, 1942	0607	Il-2		ESE of Rjev
108	Sep 14, 1942	0725	Il-2		ESE of Rjev
109		1701	Il-2		Rjev
110		1713	Il-2		
111	Sep 22, 1942	0925	MiG-3		1km NE of Klimovo
112		0931	R-5		
113	Sep 26, 1942	1233	LaGG-3		LaGG-3
114		1608	LaGG-3		LaGG-3
115	Sep 27, 1942	0659	LaGG-3		15km NE of Rjev
116		0703	LaGG-3		Klimowo
117	Nov 9, 1942	1507	Spitfire V	92 Sqn	E of Buqbuq
-		1507	Spitfire		
118	Nov 27, 1942	0732	Spitfire	1 (SAAF) Sqn	5km E of Bir el Ginn
-	Dec 7, 1942		fighter		
119	Dec 10, 1942	1505	P-40	66th FS/57th FG	10km NW of El Agheila
120	Dec 14, 1942	1508	P-40F	64th FS/57th FG	SW of El Agheila
121		1525	P-40F	64th FS/57th FG	
122	Dec 15, 1942	1058	P-40	260 (RCAF) Sqn	Ras el Aali
123	Jan 13, 1943	0845	Baltimore	21 (SAAF) Sqn	15km NE of Bir Dufan
124	Jan 14, 1943	1112	P-40	450 Sq or 1 (SAAF) Sqn	25km SE of Bir Dufan
125		1117	P-40		Bir Dufan airfield
126		1124	P-40		
127	Jan 27, 1943	1255	P-40	3 (SAAF) Sqn	10km SE of Zuara
128		1305	P-40	3 (SAAF) Sqn	30km S of Sorman
129	Jan 28, 1943	1740	P-40		5km SE of Tarhuna
130	Mar 10, 1943	1633	P-40	112 Sqn	Ksar el Hirane
131		1648	P-40	112 Sqn	Foum Tatahouine
132	Mar 13, 1943	1504	P-40	64th FS/57th FG	Matmata airfield
133		1751	P-39	64th FS/57th FG	10km NW of La Fauconnerie
134	Mar 22, 1943	1427		250 or 112 Sqn	75km SSW of Gabès
135	Mar 23, 1943	0950		2nd FS/52nd FG	40km SSW of Maknassy

Adolf Galland served as *Kommandeur* of III./JG 26 during the battle of Britain.

Oberstleutnant Adolf Galland

Adolf Galland was born on March 19, 1912, in Westerholt. His ancestors were Huguenot exiles (originally from Veynes) who fled France after the revocation of Protestant-friendly edicts. Fascinated by the exploits of the Great War flying aces, promoted in numerous publications both during World War I and post-1918, he made his first gliding flight at the age of 17 at the DLV (Deutsche Luftsportverband, the German Air Sports Federation). Shortly after receiving his *Abitur* (school-leaving certificate), he passed the entrance examination for the DFS (Deutsches Fliegerschule, the German School of Civil Aviation) in Brunswick in February 1932. However, in the summer of 1933 Galland temporarily interrupted his training as an airline pilot to take part in a military training course in Italy. He then joined Lufthansa. But his career took a decisive turn when, on February 15, 1934, he entered the Dresden

A mechanic is about to add a 50th black mark to the tailfin of Kommodore Galland's Bf 109E-4/N (W.Nr. 5819) following his victory over a Spitfire of No. 41 Squadron in the Canterbury–Maidstone sector on October 30, 1940.

Adolf Galland returns from a mission with his most famous aircraft during the battle of Britain, Bf 109E W.Nr. 5819.

Close-up of the rudder of Galland's W.Nr. 5819 with 57 victories.

Audembert, November 1940. There are now 57 victories on the rudder of Bf 109E-7/Z W.Nr. 5819, the aircraft of Obstl. Adolf Galland. However, one of the three claims of November 17 was not certified. The ace therefore did not return his 57th official *Luftsieg* until December 5. Two Bf 109E-7s can be seen in the background. His latest victim was a Hurricane of No. 249 Squadron, shot down over Dartford on November 28.

infantry school. After completing his training, Lt. Galland attended the Schlessheim aviation school, a future Luftwaffe center. As a bachelor, Oblt. "Dolfo" Galland was one of the many volunteers who went to fight in Spain. He joined the Condor Legion in May 1937 and led 3./J 88, the so-called "Mickey Mouse" *Staffel*, the last unit of the German expeditionary force to fly the He 51 biplane in the ground-attack role. Having acquired a certain reputation among his comrades as a *Draufgänger* (daredevil), Galland was unable to achieve any aerial victories in spite of the risky sorties. Returning to Germany in mid-August 1938, he helped set up the first two *Schlachtflieger* (assault aviation) groups, utilizing his Spanish experiences.

Promoted to *Kapitän* of 1./JG 52 in April 1939, Oblt. Galland was finally able to convert onto the modern Bf 109E-1. But in mid-July, he was forced to return to assault aviation, posted to 4.(S)/LG 2 based in Tutow. During the fighting in Poland in September 1939, the young officer found himself at the controls of an Hs 123 ground-attack biplane, an aircraft with which he flew a good 50 sorties until the end of the campaign. Promoted to *Hauptmann* on October 2,

This aircraft, photographed by Galland's gun camera, would have been his 57th official victim. It was a Spitfire shot down on December 5, 1940. The JG 26 ace then became the top *Tagjagd* pilot for 1940, ahead of Werner Mölders (JG 51) and Helmut Wick (JG 2).

The end of a Spitfire of No. 64 Squadron, shot down by Adolf Galland, on December 5, 1940

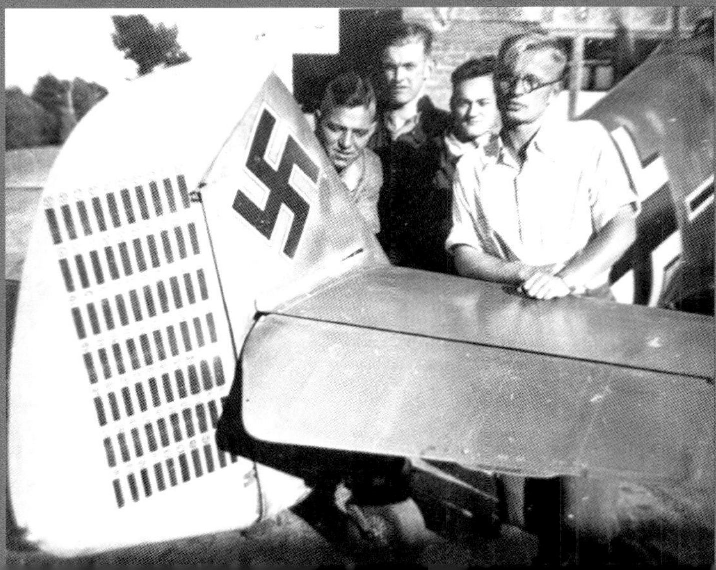

Members of the Luftwaffe and a *Feldgendarme* inspect the remains of the fuselage of one of the two Blenheims of RAF No. 226 Squadron shot down by Galland and his wingman near Merville on July 2, 1941.

The rudder of W.Nr. 6714 "DG-MV" flown by Kommodore Galland shows 70 victories. He still led the fighter pilot rankings ahead of Mölders.

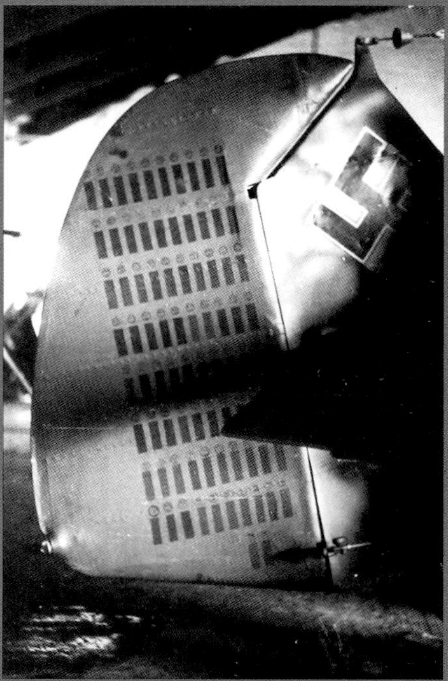

Several views of the tailfin of Galland's old Bf 109E-7 W.Nr. 5819 with 82 black bars. These pictures were taken at Cognac, home to the *Ergänzungsgruppe* of JG 26 where this particular machine had been "taken in hand" at the end of August 1941 by Hptm. Fritz Fromme, the unit's commander. "Dolfo" had returned 27 victories with this aircraft.

Audembert in the fall of 1941. This mechanic is proud to be photographed alongside the tail fin of the machine flown by the "boss." 69 is the number of victories that earned him the Swords. When this photograph was taken, he had added a further 18 successes. The last two were claimed on September 21. Note the highly polished finish of the horizontal stabilizer.

On December 5, 1941, Adolf Galland departed JG 26 following his promotion to general and Inspector of Fighters. For the occasion, Reichsmarschall Hermann Göring visited the unit and gave a speech at Audembert. In the foreground is Bf 109F-2/U W.Nr. 6750 with the No. 69 rudder decoration. Below this decoration appear Galland's next 25 successes, the last three of which were returned with this aircraft. It was modified with two 20mm MG FF/M cannon in the wings, in the manner of a Bf 109E. By this time the brand-new general had achieved 96 *Luftsiege* even though only 94 appear on his aircraft.

1939, Galland was awarded the Iron Cross 2nd Class. On February 10, 1940, he was finally and definitively assigned to the day fighter arm when he joined the Stab/JG 27 at Krefeld.

On May 10, 1940, *Westfeldzug* was launched. On the morning of May 12, Galland shot down his first aircraft, Hurricanes, to the west of the Liège. By the end of the *Westfeldzug*, he had won 14 victories. His successes propelled him to the head of III./JG 26 on June 11, 1940 (although the campaign was not quite over). On August 22, he was promoted again: Hptm. Galland was named *Kommodore* of JG 26 "Schlageter." At only 28 he was the leading scorer in three months of fighting against the RAF and the Armée de l'Air. On July 29, 1940, he was awarded the Knight's Cross after 17 victories. On November 1, 1940, Kommodore Galland was promoted to *Oberstleutnant*.

JG 26 was deployed over England during the remainder of 1940 (except for a few rest periods). Through early 1941, JG 26 "stood guard" against the RAF on the Channel front. As Luftwaffe units gradually deserted the west to shift to the Balkans and then Central Europe, JG 26 remained in France with JG 2 facing the RAF.

On June 21, 1941, on the eve of *Barbarossa*, the *Kommodore* brought his total to 69 victories and was subsequently awarded the Swords to his Knight's Cross for this milestone. In order to keep pressure on the Luftwaffe in France and Belgium and aware ot its weakness, the RAF launched its "Non-Stop Offensive" in June. Numerous raids and sweeps took place over the continent, which allowed Galland to gradually increase his victory scoreboard. With 96 successes in the air, all of them on the Western Front, Adolf Galland was appointed to succeed the late Werner Mölders as Inspector of Fighters. This appointment would take him away from the front lines while at the same time enabling him to tour all the different theaters. In 1944, he was the youngest and most highly decorated general in Germany, wearing the Knight's Cross with Oak Leaves, Swords, and Diamonds. According to some sources, although he was banned from flying, he "unofficially" flew some 10 combat sorties with a small autonomous unit in the *Reichsverteidigung* (defense of the Reich) and even shot down two *Viermots* at the controls of an Fw 190A on March 8, 1944.

The glory days were followed by years of crisis. Defeat threatened and tensions increased. Relations with his superiors deteriorated and Galland was almost arrested for insubordination at the end of 1944. Following the personal intervention of Adolf Hitler, Galland was tasked with raising a new fighter unit to demonstrate the capabilities of the new Me 262 jet fighters. In early April 1945, Galland officially went back into action against the USAAF. He returned seven more victories, ending the war with 103 *Abschüsse*.

Interrogated at length by the victorious Allies, Galland was quickly freed and left shortly thereafter for Argentina, at the invitation of General Juan Peron. Together with Dr Kurt Tank, he developed the FMA IA 58 Pulqui II for the benefit of the Fuerza Aerea Argentina. Back in Germany, the former general worked as a consultant in the aerospace industry, benefiting from the renown he had gained from his biographical work *Die Ersten und die Letzten* (*The First and the Last*). The Luftwaffe's former fighter general died of cardiac arrest on February 9, 1996. Galland's three brothers were all in the Luftwaffe. Paul, a pilot in 8./JG 26, was killed over the Channel in combat with a Spitfire on October 31, 1942 (he had 17victories to his credit). Wilhelm-Ferdinand ("Wutz") was shot down on August 17, 1943 by a P-47 while leading II./JG 26 (he was credited with 55 victories and wore the Knight's Cross). Friedrich ("Fritz") likewise entered the Jagdwaffe but had a less than distinguished career as a fighter pilot, prior to being transferred to reconnaissance *Staffeln*, including 2./NAG 11, a unit that flew operations over Italy in 1944.

Galland's victories

No	Date	Time	Aircraft	Unit	Place
1	May 12, 1940		Hurricane	87 Squadron	nr Liège
2	May 12, 1940		Hurricane	87 Squadron	nr Liège
3	May 12, 1940		Hurricane		nr Liège
4	May 16, 1940		Spitfire		nr Lille
5	May 19, 1940		Potez		N Albert
6	May 19, 1940		Potez		SW Hirson
7	May 20, 1940		Potez		S Amiens
8	May 29, 1940		Blenheim		Gravelines
9	May 29, 1940		Blenheim		Gravelines
10	Jun 2, 1940		Spitfire		W Dunkerque
11	June 9, 1940		H-75		W Rotoy
12	June 9, 1940		MS 406		nr Meaux
13	Jun 14, 1940		Blenheim		nr Vernon
14	Jun 14, 1940		Fairey Battle		nr Evreux
15	Jul 24, 1940		Spitfire	54 Squadron	nr Margate
16	Jul 25, 1940		Spitfire	54 Squadron	nr Dover Harbour
17	Jul 28, 1940		Spitfire	74 Squadron	nr Dover
18	Aug 12, 1940		Hurricane	501 Squadron	nr Margate
19	Aug 14, 1940		Hurricane	32 or 615 Squadron	S Dover
20	Aug 15, 1940		Spitfire	54 or 64 Squadron	Dover/Folkestone
21	Aug 15, 1940		Spitfire	54 or 64 Squadron	Dover/Folkestone
22	Aug 15, 1940		Spitfire	54 or 64 Squadron	Dover/Folkestone
23	Aug 25, 1940		Spitfire	610 or 616 Squadron	Dungeness/Folkestone
24	Aug 28, 1940		Defiant	264 Squadron	Faversham
25	Aug 31, 1940		Spitfire	19 Squadron	Cambridge/Gravesend
26	Aug 31, 1940		Spitfire		Cambridge/Gravesend
27	Aug 31, 1940		Hurricane		Cambridge/Gravesend
28	Sep 1, 1940		Spitfire	79 or 85 Squadron	London
29	Sep 3, 1940		Hurricane	257 Squadron	Chelmsford
30	Sep 6, 1940		Hurricane	601 Squadron	Tonbridge
31	Sep 11, 1940		Hurricane	501 Squadron	NW Dingeness
32	Sep 14, 1940		Hurricane	253 Squadron	S London
33	Sep 15, 1940		Hurricane	301 Squadron	Thames estuary
34	Sep 18, 1940		Hurricane	46 Squadron	Rochester
35	Sep 18, 1940		Hurricane	46 Squadron	Rochester
36	Sep 18, 1940		Hurricane	46 Squadron	Rochester

37	Sep 20, 1940		Spitfire	222 Squadron	S Hornchurch
38	Sep 21, 1940		Spitfire	92 Squadron	Ashford/Canterbury
39	Sep 23, 1940		Hurricane	257 Squadron	N Rochester
40			Hurricane		
41	Sep 24, 1940		Hurricane	17 Squadron	Rochester
42	Sep 30, 1940		Hurricane	303 Squadron	S Guildford
43	Oct 8, 1940		Spitfire	66 Squadron	S Eastchurch
44	Oct 11, 1940		Spitfire	421 Flight	Chatham
45			Hurricane	253 Squadron	Rochester
46	Oct 15, 1940		Spitfire		S Rochester
47	Oct 26, 1940		Hurricane		S London
48	Oct 30, 1940		Spitfire	222 Squadron	between London and Maidstone
49			Spitfire	41 Squadron	
50			Spitfire	41 Squadron	
51	Nov 1, 1940		Spitfire	74 Squadron	nr Ashford
52	Nov 14, 1940		Spitfire	66 or 74 Squadron	S Dover
53	Nov 15, 1940		Hurricane	605 Squadron	Dover
54	Nov 17, 1940		Hurricane	17 Squadron	Harwich
55			Hurricane	257 Squadron	
56			Hurricane	257 Squadron	
57	Nov 28, 1940		Hurricane	249 Squadron	Dartford
58	Dec 5, 1940		Spitfire	64 Squadron	Dover/Dungeness
59	Apr 4, 1941		Spitfire	91 Squadron	Dover/Canterbury
60	Apr 15, 1941		Spitfire	Wittering Wing	Dover area
61			Spitfire	266 Squadron	
62	Jun 13, 1941		Hurricane	56 or 242 Squadron	Dover/Ashford
63			Hurricane	56 or 242 Squadron	
64	Jun 16, 1941		Hurricane	258 Squadron	W Boulogne
65	Jun 17, 1941		Hurricane	56 or 242 Squadron	W Saint-Omer
66			Hurricane	56 or 242 Squadron	
67	Jun 18, 1941		Spitfire	145 Squadron	nr Ardres
68	Jun 21, 1941		Blenheim	21 Squadron	Lumbres and Etaples
69			Blenheim	21 Squadron	
-	Jun 21, 1941		Blenheim		nr Merville
70	Jul 2, 1941		Blenheim	226 Squadron	nr Merville

71	Jul 23, 1941		Spitfire		Gravelines
72			Spitfire		Bruges
73			Spitfire		Bruges
74	Aug 7, 1941		Spitfire		Lumbres
75			Spitfire		nr Saint-Omer
76	Aug 9, 1941		Spitfire	452 Squadron	nr Saint-Pol
-	Aug 9, 1941		Spitfire		nr Ardres
77	Aug 12, 1941		Blenheim	19 or 152 Squadron	Flushing (Vlissingen) area
78			Spitfire	19 or 152 Squadron	
79	Aug 19, 1941		Spitfire	111 Squadron	Bergues/Gravelines
80			Spitfire	452 Squadron	
81			Hurricane	71 Squadron	
82	Sep 4, 1941		Blenheim	18 Squadron	N Saint-Omer
83	Sep 7, 1941		Spitfire	71 Squadrom	W Boulogne
84	Sep 20, 1941		Spitfire		Bergues area
85			Spitfire		
86	Sep 21, 1941		Spitfire	Tangmere Wing	Etaples/Dunkirk
87			Spitfire	111 Squadron	
88	Oct 13, 1941		Spitfire	139 Squadron	Saint-Omer/Samer
89			Blenheim		
90	Oct 21, 1941		Spitfire	611 Squadron	Samer/Boulogne
91			Spitfire		
92			Spitfire		
93	Oct 27, 1941		Spitfire	401 Squadron	S Dunkirk
94	Nov 8, 1941		Spitfire	315 Squadron	Montreuil/Hazebrouck
95			Spitfire	316 Squadron	
96	Nov 18, 1941		Spitfire	602 Squadron	W Boulogne
97	end 1944		B-24		
98			B-24		
-	Apr 3, 1945		P-38		
99	Apr 5, 1945		B-24		
100	Apr 16, 1945		B-26		Landsberg-am-Lech
101			B-26		
102	Apr 21, 1945		B-17		
103	Apr 26, 1945		B-26		Munich-Riem
104			B-26		

Hauptmann Franz von Werra

Born on July 13, 1914, in Leuck, Switzerland, into an impoverished noble family, François Gustave de Werra was adopted by a family friend, Baroness Luisa von Haber, whose nationality and name he took. He was raised with one of his sisters in Bueron, Kreis Sigmaringen, in southern Germany. At the age of 10, the boy escaped from the strictness of the Baroness von Haber and embarked as a ship's boy and travelled to New Orleans. This trip stimulated his appetite for adventure and strengthened his character. When he returned home, he received a cold reception from the family, but his school welcomed him back with open arms. Later on, he worked at odd jobs such as a gardener and a locksmith. When he came of age, he elected to take back his real name and François de Werra became Franz von Werra. During his military service in 1934, he quickly applied for the air force. His vitality, his daredevil temperament and his individualism made him suitable for the fighter arm. After his training, he was seriously injured in an accident in March 1939 at Königsberg airfield. The plane buried its nose in the ground, but fortunately did not catch fire. Unable to move, the pilot was taken to hospital with spinal injuries. His flying career seemed to be over. During his convalescence he met Elfi Traut, a young girl introduced to him by his commander, the ace Wilhelm Bathasar. He married her two years later. Fully recovered by the time war was declared, Franz von Werra was able to serve in Poland (probably in I./JG 77) before being

Oblt. Franz von Werra, *Gruppenadjutant* of II./JG 3, with Simba the lion cub in the cockpit of his "Emil."

On August 28, 1940, von Werra claimed to have a carried out a daring solitary attack on a formation of Hurricanes over Kent, shooting down three as they were setting up for a landing and then strafing and destroying five machines on the ground. Despite a lack of witnesses, von Werra's claims were apparently accepted as his victories 6–8, at least at unit level, making August 28 the most successful day for I./JG 3 during the battle of Britain. Here his latest successes are being painted on the tailfin of his Bf 109E.

transferred to the Stab II./JG 3 which was then being formed. On May 19, 1940, this *Gruppe* deployed to France. The following day, von Werra scored his first victory (a Hurricane of No. 85 Squadron. near Arras) and then obtained an astonishing hattrick on Wednesday 22nd (two Breguet 693s of GBA I/51 and a Potez 63 of GBA II/51). On May 26, he became an ace by downing a Hurricane of No. 605 Squadron over Dunkirk. On August 28, 1940, in the late afternoon over England, he was credited with a Spitfire of No. 603 or 610 Squadron and two Hurricanes of No. 56 Squadron near Rochester, as well as five aircraft destroyed on the ground—all in one sortie! He filed the following mission report:

> I was flying as the *Kommandeur*'s wingman as part of the *Stabsschwarm* when we attacked a formation of about 20 Hawker Hurricanes. Their formation and then ours dispersed and we fought individually. I was involved in a dogfight with a Spitfire belonging to a second unit which attacked us just after the start of the battle. The Englishman hit my aircraft, destroying my radio. We lost a great deal of altitude while maneuvering into a firing position and had descended to 2,000 meters before I finally managed to take aim. My adversary was hit and immediately dived. I plunged behind him while firing more bursts, but he did not pull out and crashed three kilometers west of Rochester.
>
> Flying again in the direction of the mouth of the Thames at very low altitude, I noticed six single-engined aircraft on my left. They had their landing gear down and were in a curve, preparing to land. I looked hard and saw ahead and below them a runway half hidden by a cloud of dust. Another formation was landing. At this time, I was only 300–500 meters behind the first group I had seen, so I also put my landing gear down and, with my engine throttled back, positioned myself behind the last aircraft which I identified as a Hurricane. As I circled over the runway like the seventh machine in

Barely a week later, on September 5, after an escort mission, he was bounced by Spitfires and forced to belly-land his damaged 109 at Winchet Hill, south of London. This is his Bf 109E-4, W.Nr. 1480 down on English soil. Note the black/white segmented spinner.

the landing pattern, I could leisurely observe the airfield's dispersal area with aircraft parked under trees to the west of the runway. I did not see any anti-aircraft defenses. My formation began to land. As the first three machines lined up towards the runway and lost altitude, I retracted my wheels, opened up my engine and fired a burst at the aircraft immediately ahead of me. Instantaneously, it fell on fire. Maneuvering, I placed myself behind the second Englishman and easily shot him down in flames.

I continued to fly in the direction of the runway and then made a climbing turn to gain altitude, finally firing into the dispersal where I could just see the rudder tips of some Hurricanes protruding above the tops of their blast pens. I fired at the first aircraft, but my height did not enable me to aim at the rest. A little farther away I saw a bowser with two Hurricanes parked on its right and another on its left. I fired at the bowser which exploded, setting flre to all three aircraft. Keeping at low altitude I made a half-turn away from the

Von Werra's scoreboard: eight air victories and five planes destroyed on the ground (arrows pointing down).

Von Werra replaced Oblt. Wilfried Balfanz as *Kommandeur* I./JG 53 and was promoted to *Hauptmann*. He achieved his first victory on the Eastern Front on July 6, 1941, and this view of his rudder scoreboard towards the end of July 1941 shows that his claims ultimately bore little relation to his credited victory total.

One of the last pictures of von Werra. He left Russia in mid-August 1941 to get married.

> installations before carrying out a further attack. This time I tried to destroy the aircraft parked in the blast pens but was unable to observe any hits. The anti-aircraft defenses were practically non-existent, with only a few machine-guns opening fire, but I dived towards them and forced the troops to run for shelter. I made two more attacks from different directions and set another aircraft on fire in its pen. That made five Hurricanes on fire on the airfield. A tent [possibly reserved for aircraft maintenance] was also burning. Constant bursts now came up towards me from guns on the edges of the aerodrome, and I carried out my last attack against some of them. I then turned 90° towards the north, joined the mouth of the Thames and recrossed the English Channel.

On the morning of September 5, 1940, the Luftwaffe launched an attack on Biggin Hill airfield, but first carried out a diversionary raid on Croydon to induce the British fighters to pull back from Biggin Hill. Thirty Messerschmitts belonging to II/JG 3 took part in this surprise raid. Leading the formation was Hptm. Erich von Selle. A *Rotte* comprising his two staff officers covered him in the air: Lt. Heinrich Sanneman (TO, *technische Offizier*, technical officer) flew on the left position and Oblt. Franz von Werra, second officer, on the right. Five minutes after the bombing of Croydon, three Spitfires of No. 603 Squadron emerged out of the sun and attacked. If von Selle was lucky enough to dive at the right moment, von Werra was hit by a burst of fire as he turned to follow his leader. He immediately reversed his 109 in the opposite direction to his comrades and dove violently. Pursued by Flt Lt Clarence Paterson Hughes's Spitfire, von Werra was then forced to make a crash landing in a field south of Maidstone, Kent. He was taken captive. However, his only thought was to escape. Three attempts failed. Sent to Canada, he jumped off the train on January 24, 1941, in the middle of a blizzard and, with frozen ears and feet, managed to reach the still-neutral United States. The escapee was taken in charge by sympathizers who took him to Brazil. He reached Barcelona on April 16. Back in Berlin he was awarded the Knight's Cross on December 14 (for some unknown reason, given his "only" eight victories). After writing a book about his adventures, *Mein Flucht aus England* (*My Escape from England*), a publication censored as "pro-British"—the author simply avoided ideological clichés—he returned to service with the Tagjagd. Eager to prove himself, he obtained a transfer to the Eastern Front as *Kommandeur* of I./JG 53 during *Barbarossa*. His aerial prowess resulted in 13 victories (two unconfirmed aircraft) in the USSR in July 1941, bringing his tally to 19.

In August, von Werra's *Gruppe* was withdrawn from the front to be re-equipped with the Bf 109F-4. The *Kommandeur* took advantage of a spell of leave to marry his Austrian fiancée and then left for the Netherlands. His *Gruppe* was tasked with the defense of the North Sea coast. On October 25, near Katwijk, Hptm. von Werra crashed into the sea in front of his pilots, presumably due to a technical failure of his Bf 109F-4/Z "double chevron" W.Nr. 7285. Despite a search, no trace of the aircraft or its pilot was ever found. Just before attempting to ditch his "Friedrich," he is said to have radioed his colleagues: "*Verdammt kalt zum Baden, was*?" ("A bit cold for a swim, eh?"). He was 27 years old when he died.

Von Werra's victories

<table>
<tr><th>No</th><th>Date</th><th>Time</th><th>Aircraft</th><th>Unit</th><th>Place</th></tr>
<tr><td>1</td><td>May 20, 1940</td><td></td><td>Hurricane</td><td>85 Sqn</td><td>15km east of Arras</td></tr>
<tr><td>2</td><td rowspan="3">May 22, 1940</td><td></td><td>Breguet 690</td><td rowspan="2">GBA I/51</td><td rowspan="3">nr Cambrai</td></tr>
<tr><td>3</td><td></td><td>Breguet 690</td></tr>
<tr><td>4</td><td></td><td>Potez 63</td><td></td></tr>
<tr><td>5</td><td>May 26, 1940</td><td></td><td>Hurricane</td><td>605 Sqn</td><td>vicinity of Dunkirk</td></tr>
<tr><td>-</td><td>Jun 3, 1940</td><td></td><td>Morane 406</td><td></td><td rowspan="3">3km west of Rochester</td></tr>
<tr><td>6</td><td rowspan="3">Aug 28, 1940</td><td></td><td>Spitfire</td><td>603 ou 610 Sqn</td></tr>
<tr><td>7</td><td></td><td>Hurricane</td><td rowspan="2">56 Sqn</td></tr>
<tr><td>8</td><td></td><td>Hurricane</td><td></td></tr>
<tr><td>9</td><td>Jul 7, 1941</td><td></td><td>DB-3</td><td></td><td>S of Ploskirow</td></tr>
<tr><td>10</td><td>Jul 8, 1941</td><td></td><td>DB-3</td><td></td><td></td></tr>
<tr><td>11</td><td rowspan="2">Jul 11, 1941</td><td></td><td>"SB-3" (SB2 bis)</td><td></td><td rowspan="2">Kudno</td></tr>
<tr><td>12</td><td></td><td>"SB-3" (SB2 bis)</td><td></td></tr>
<tr><td>13</td><td>Jul 12, 1941</td><td></td><td>DB-3</td><td></td><td></td></tr>
<tr><td>14</td><td>Jul 17, 1941</td><td></td><td>I-153</td><td></td><td></td></tr>
<tr><td>15</td><td>Jul 18, 1941</td><td></td><td>DB-3</td><td></td><td></td></tr>
<tr><td>-</td><td>Jul 23, 1941</td><td></td><td>2 x enemy a/c</td><td></td><td></td></tr>
<tr><td>16</td><td>Jul 26, 1941</td><td></td><td>B-3</td><td></td><td></td></tr>
<tr><td>17</td><td>Jul 29, 1941</td><td></td><td>B-3</td><td></td><td>S of Smola</td></tr>
<tr><td>18</td><td rowspan="2">Jul 31, 1941</td><td></td><td>Pe-2 twins</td><td></td><td></td></tr>
<tr><td>19</td><td></td><td>Pe-2 twins</td><td></td><td></td></tr>
</table>

Major Josef Wurmheller

Born on May 4, 1917, in Hausham, this Bavarian aviation enthusiast already had his glider and pilot licenses in 1935. In 1937, he began his training as a fighter pilot with the Luftwaffe before being transferred to 2./JG 53. After having obtained his first victory in the "Phoney War," he was required to train young pilots and left for a few months to serve as an instructor in a fighter school. Back to the "Pik Ace" during the battle of Britain, "Sepp" Wurmheller would carve out a reputation but would also be forced to bail out several times over the Channel, being rescued mostly unscathed on each occasion. Nevertheless, he spent the winter of 1940/1 in hospital after his last landing. In March 1941, he returned to JG 53, won a few victories over the Channel front and then followed

Fw. Wurmheller photographed alongside his II./JG 53 Bf 109F-2 "Black 3" W.Nr. 5434 in the East, July 1941. Note that a yellow theater band has yet to be painted on the machine.

Mechanic Willy Preushammer alongside the rudder decoration on Ofw. Wurmheller's Fw 19C "White 3," late August 1942. Several victories already marked up from June would not be confirmed.

his unit to the USSR where he added a dozen *Luftsiegen* to his list of achievements. In July 1941, Wurmheller had to be one of the pilots who, according to a letter from a JG 3 aviator, "with at least three victories and having previously taken part in engagements over England, were designated by each *Gruppe* operating in the East to return to the West." It is likely that, in view of his victories, Wurmheller had in fact volunteered to return to the Channel front. He was thus posted to II./JG 2 and continued to score victories. After 32 *Abschüsse*, he was awarded the Knight's Cross on September 4, 1941. He then left the Channel front for a period of six months, again to serve as an instructor at a fighter training school. Returning to action in May 1942, Wurmheller took part in several hard-fought dogfights such as those on August 19, 1942, over Dieppe. On November 13, 1942, he received the Oak Leaves after his 60th victory while being appointed *Leutnant as Tapferkeitsoffizier* (officer by courage).

On September 23, 1943, Wurmheller was seriously injured during a bombing raid on the airfield at Vannes. Airborne to counter a 1st BD raid on Nantes the *Staffelkapitän* of 9./ JG 2 had just landed when the airfield came under attack. According to one eyewitness account Wurmheller's machine was obliterated by a direct hit. "Sepp" had just vacated the cockpit but was seriously wounded by shrapnel. 9./ JG 2 mechanic Ogfr. Willi Kittel reported: "He was lying unconscious on the ground. We loaded him into our ambulance and took off at top speed for the hospital in Vannes. When he returned to the *Staffel* two months later he had an enormous scar on the side of his head that ran down to his neck."

On June 9, 1944, Wurmheller was appointed *Kommandeur* of III./JG 2 and returned his 100th victory one week later. On June 22, 1944, credited with 102 victories, he was killed in action over Alençon. He would be promoted to *Major* and receive the Swords posthumously. He also had to his credit the destruction of about 20 four-engined aircraft.

This photo poses a conundrum. While he appears to be wearing the Oak Leaves, obtained for his 60 victories, Wurmheller is here alongside a rudder displaying 49 *Abschüsse* (including nine victories over Soviet machines). Could this be an "old" rudder affixed to another aircraft?

Lt. Wurmheller, wearing the Oak Leaves, alongside his rudder displaying 73 victories. The scoreboard dates this photo to late April 1943 (68 of these would be confirmed). Around 1942, the great aces tended to have their rudders repainted when they received a high decoration, usually comprising a representation of the award and the number of victories achieved in attaining it—in this case it was 60 for the Oak Leaves. Further victory bars were then added below this "summary." Note here the appearance of the first American aircraft (identified by the white stars) and the "doubles" won by Wurmheller.

Pilots of 9./JG 2 alongside Wurmheller's Fw 190A-5 "Yellow 2" W.Nr. 7334 following combat on the evening of June 28, 1943 when 158 B-17s attacked locks and submarine pens at Saint-Nazaire between 1655 and 1725. Airborne from Vannes, III./JG 2 claimed 13 B-17s, although possibly four of these were duplicates. Uffz. Swat (first left) has just recorded his second victory, while Wurmheller is fourth left glancing at his rudder which shows 80 victories. The experienced Fw. Karl-Heinz Munsche is third left. W.Nr. 7334 was destroyed in a taxiing accident on July 29, 1943, at Vannes.

In late August 1943 propaganda company photographer Engelmann was in Vannes, France, to take pictures of Oblt. Josef Wurmheller posing alongside his new Fieseler-manufactured Fw 190A-6 "Yellow 2" W.Nr. 530314 There are 78 victory bars on the yellow rudder scoreboard; his 78th was a Spitfire shot down during the evening of August 22, 1943. It is a challenge to keep tabs on Wurmheller's tally from his rudder scoreboards—his previous mount, Fw 190A-5, "Yellow 2" W.Nr. 7334—displayed 80 victories.

Oblt. Josef Wurmheller's III./JG 2 Fw 190 A-5, "Yellow 2" W.Nr. 7334. Wurmheller was shot down and killed by Mustangs over the Normandy "Invasionsfront" on June 22, 1944.

Wurmheller's victories

No	Date	Time	Aircraft	Unit	Place
1	Sep 30, 1939	1210	Fairey Battle	150 Squadron	Ecury-sur-Coole
2	Sep 28, 1940	1345	Spitfire		
3	Sep 30, 1940	1743	Hurricane	87 Sqn	
4	Oct 12, 1940	1215	Spitfire		NW Brest
5	Oct 16, 1940	1520	Blenheim		NE Ouessant
6	Apr 4, 1941	1118	Spitfire		W Wissant
7	Apr 9, 1941	1721	Spitfire		Dover Straits
8	Apr 10, 1941	1843	Blenheim		
9	May 7, 1941	0747	Spitfire		
10		0747	Spitfire		
11	Jun 22, 1941	-	SB-3	VVS-ZOVO	N Tauroggen
12	Jun 23, 1941	0900	SB-3	VVS Northwestern Front	nr Tauroggen
13	Jul 1, 1941	1950	SB-3	VVS Northwestern Front	
14	Jul 4, 1941	1452	SB-3	VVS Northwestern Front	Ostrov area
15	Jul 6, 1941	1945	SB-3	VVS Northwestern Front	between Pleskau and Ostrov
16		1947	SB-3	VVS Northwestern Front	
17	Jul 11, 1941	0325	I-16	VVS Northwestern Front	Ostrov area
18	Jul 12, 1941	1946	SB-3	VVS Northwestern Front	Ostrov area
19	Jul 15, 1941	1835	SB-3	VVS Northwestern Front	Ostrov area
20	Jul 24, 1941	1225	Spitfire		Hazebrouck
21	Aug 7, 1941	0752	Spitfire	N°485, 602 or 611 Sqn	
22		1747	Spitfire	N°485, 602 or 611 Sqn	
23	Aug 16, 1941	1940	Spitfire	N° 609 Sqn	
24	Aug 18, 1941	1605	Spitfire		Lille/Calais
25		1616	Spitfire		
26	Aug 21, 1941	1508	Spitfire		
27	Aug 26, 1941	1923	Spitfire		
28		1924	Spitfire		
29	Aug 27, 1941	0930	Spitfire		Thérane
30	Aug 29, 1941	0830	Spitfire		
31	Sep 4, 1941	1738	Spitfire		Saint-Omer/Béthune
32	May 17, 1941	1402	Spitfire		
33	May 19, 1941	2045	Spitfire	N°174 or 350 Sqn	NW Calais
34		2047	Spitfire	N°174 or 350 Sqn	
35		2049	Spitfire	N°174 or 350 Sqn	

36	May 30, 1942	2130	Spitfire		
37		2130	Spitfire		
38	May 31, 1942	1932	Spitfire	N°133 or 485 Sqn	
39		1933	Spitfire	N°133 or 485 Sqn	
40		1935	Spitfire	N°133 or 485 Sqn	
41		1937	Spitfire	N°133 or 485 Sqn	
42	Jun 2, 1942	1058	Spitfire	N°403 Sqn	off Dieppe/Tréport
43		1100	Spitfire	N°403 Sqn	
44		1104	Spitfire	N°403 Sqn	
45	Jun 3, 1942	1647	Spitfire	N°154 or 312 Sqn	off Le Havre
46		1650	Spitfire	N°154 or 312 Sqn	
47	Jun 5, 1942	1545	Spitfire	N°128, 133 or 401 Sqn	Abbeville canal
48		1545	Spitfire	N°128, 133 or 401 Sqn	
49		1546	Spitfire	N°128, 133 or 401 Sqn	
50		1546	Spitfire	N°128, 133 or 401 Sqn	
51	Jun 20, 1942	1551	Spitfire	N°129 or 340 Sqn	off Le Havre
52		1552	Spitfire	N°129 or 340 Sqn	
53	Aug 19, 1942	0908	Spitfire		nr Dieppe
54		0912	Spitfire		
55		0916	Spitfire	N°88 Sqn	
56		1516	Spitfire		
57		1517	Spitfire		
58		1732	Spitfire		
59		1845	Blenheim/ Baltimore		
60	Aug 20, 1942	1902	Spitfire		N Caen
-		1904	Spitfire		
61	Sep 8, 1942	1439	Spitfire	N°302 Sqn	off Le Havre
62	Oct 2, 1942	1543	Spitfire	N° 401 Sqn	N Fécamp
63	Oct 31, 1942	1808	Spitfire		SW Canterbury
64		1812	Spitfire		SE Walmer
65	Feb 16, 1943	1115	B-17	303rd, 305th or 306th BG	N Brittany
66		1118	B-17	303rd, 305th or 306th BG	
67	Mar 12, 1943	1311	Typhoon		N Fécamp
68	Apr 16, 1943	1425	B-17	305th BG	

69	May 1, 1943	1130	B-17	427th BS/303rd BG	W Saint Nazaire
70	May 17, 1943	1213	B-17	305th or 385th G	SE Lorient
71	May 29, 1943	1625	B-17	410th BS/94th BG	near Pontorson
72		1627	B-17	410th BS/94th BG	near Pontorson
73	Jun 28, 1943	1710	B-17	351st BG	SW Escoublac
74	Jul 4, 1943	1309	B-17		off Saint-Nazaire
75		1311	B-17		off Saint-Nazaire
76	Jul 10, 1943	0815	B-17		SW Berck-sur-Mer
77	Aug 3, 1943	2026	Spitfire		NE Brest
78	Aug 16, 1943	1228	Spitfire		S Fruer
79	Aug 22, 1943	1950	Spitfire		SE Tricqueville
80	Aug 27, 1943	0946	Spitfire		Octeville
81	Sep 2, 1943	1905	P-47		near Neufchâtael
82	Sep 3, 1943	0947	B-17		S Villacoublay
83		1048	B-17		off Octeville
84	Sep 15, 1943	1941	B-17		Saint-Germain-en-Laye
85		1946	B-17		
86	Jan 29, 1944	1104	B-24		N Charleville
87	Feb 8, 1944	1026	B-17		Crèvecoeur/Le Tréport
88	Feb 24, 1944	1420	B-24		E Fürsteneau
89	Feb 25, 1944	1126	B-26		off Knokke
-		1128	B-26		
90		1528	B-17		Mondorf-les-Bains
91	Mar 2, 1944	1135	B-17		Charleville
92	Mar 16, 1944	1040	B-17		Saint-Dizier
93	Apr 10, 1944	0926	B-17		Dormans
94		0928	P-38		
95	Apr 12, 1944	1315	B-24		
96	Jun 7, 1944	0603	Typhoon	N°197 Sqn	Bayeux, Normandy
97	Jun 8, 1944	0925	P-51		NE Caen
98	Jun 12, 1944	1044	P-47		NW Lisieux
99		1048	P-47		SW Caen
100	Jun 16, 1944	2004	P-51		between Caen and Lisieux

Hauptmann Frank Liesendahl

Born in Wuppertal-Barmen on February 23, 1915, Frank Liesendahl was serving in a front-line Luftwaffe unit as early as 1937 (probably in JG 133). In 1939, he was transferred to 5./ZG 1 and flew in the Polish campaign. Back in the Reich, his group adopted the deception name of J.Gr. 101 while waiting to receive Bf 110s. In late December Lt. Liesendahl was posted to 4./JG 2 having probably expressed a wish not to fly twin-engined aircraft. He flew with this *Staffel* during the campaign in the West. On May 26, 1940, having been appointed adjutant of II./JG 2, he was shot down in combat in the Calais sector but remained in French captivity for only four days, being freed by advancing German forces. Although wounded and hospitalized for a while, Liesendahl returned to the "Richthofen." Promoted to *Oberleutnant*, he took command of 6. Staffel on September 9, 1940, and fought over England as well as during the "Non-Stop Offensive" of 1941.

Perhaps not unsurprisingly, commanding a *Staffel* that specialized in *Jabo* attacks (fighter-bombers), Liesendahl failed to claim any air victories and may well have preferred the fighter-bomber *Jabo* mission. Operating "Emils" and then "Friedrichs," Liesendahl's 6. Staffel took off with a bomb slung on a belly rack and a large escort of "classic" fighters before diving on their targets, most often a ship that had ventured into the Channel. Between May 17 and 23 June 23, Liesendahl claimed—alone or in cooperation—the sinking of three merchant ships of between 2,500 and 10,000 gross tonnage (GRT). On July 10, 1941, during a fiercely disputed battle, Oblt. Liesendahl was wounded and hospitalized for two months.

At the end of his convalescence, he was posted to the Luftwaffe test center at Rechlin to evaluate the Fw 190 and to share his experience of *Jabo* operations with the specialists. As one of the foremost combat pilots in this type of mission, he laid out the tactics he had devised: the so-called "Liesendahl *Verfahren*." On his return to the unit, he supported the idea of a single *Staffel* of *Jabos* dedicated solely to this task and with motivated pilots.

Lt. Liesendahl at Nordholz in early 1940, shortly after his arrival at 4./JG 2.

Operating in the *Jabo* role, 6./JG 2 Friedrich's featured an appropriate emblem on the yellow-painted cowls—a small figure seated astride a bomb. This would be replaced by the red fox design in March 1942

Initially called the Jabo Staffel of Luftflotte 3, this unit was created on November 10, 1941 and redesignated 13.(Jabo)/JG 2 on February 17, 1942, then 10.(Jabo)/JG 2, operating under the control of the "Richthofen." Based at Beaumont-le-Roger, the *Staffel* adopted a very telling badge: a red fox carrying a ship in its mouth; earning the unit the nickname of the "*Rote Füchse*."

A number of sorties were mounted but, on July 17, 1942 off Brixham, 13./JG 2 lost its first aircraft: that of its *Staffelkapitän* which crashed at sea, victim of anti-aircraft fire from the tanker *Daxhound*. Liesendahl was making his 142nd combat flight that day at the controls of Fw 190A-2 W.Nr. 0439 "Blue 14." Two days later, his body was pulled from the sea by the crew of a British ship and, after identification, buried at sea. On September 4, 1942, Liesendahl was posthumously awarded the Knight's Cross.

On March 31, 1942, Oblt. Liesendahl placed a bomb on target on a 4 000-ton ship as indicated by the rudder of his Bf 109F-4/B W.Nr. 7629 "Blue 7." His scoreboard also shows successes on May 17, June 9, and 23, 1941, and March 23 and 27, 1942. However, the March 24, 1942, strike does not appear, having probably not yet been credited.

Bf 109 F-4/B W.Nr. 7629 "Blue 1" of 10.(Jabo) / JG 2 flown by Oblt. Frank Liesendahl. Liesendahl was KIA on July 17, 1942, shot down into the sea by anti-aircraft fire while attacking shipping off the south coast of England.

Oblt. Liesendahl observing the rudder of his W.Nr. 7629 after his success on April 25, 1942. This machine was subsequently renumbered as "Blue 1."

Liesendahl's victories

No	Date	Time	Vessel	Place	Comments
1	May 17, 1941	1600	freighter 2,500 BRT	off Brighton	with other pilots
2	Jun 9, 1941	1500	freighter of 5,000 BRT	off Swanage	
3	Jun 23, 1941	1245	armed freighter 10,000 BRT	in the Channel	
4	Mar 23, 1942		steamer of 3,000 BRT	off Newhaven	with Lt Nippa and Lt Fröschl
5	Mar 24, 1942		freighter of 2,000		with Oblt Schröter and Lt Nippa
6	Mar 27, 1942		BRT steamer of 3,000 BRT	Paignton harbor	with Lt. Nippa
7	Mar 31, 1942		freighter *London City* of 3,000 BRT		damaged
8	Apr 25, 1942		ship of 3,000/4,000 BRT	off Solent Ham	with Lt Fröschl and Uffz Schwarzer
9	May 2, 1942		ship of 2,500 BRT	Seaford harbor	with Lt Fröschl
10	Jul 7, 1942		ship of 10,000 BRT	off the Solent	damaged with Oblt Schröter
11	Jul 11, 1942		destroyer		SE of Dartmouth

Liesendahl shares a drink with Major Walter Oesau, *Kommodore* of JG 2 during May 1942. Oesau was a Knight's Cross holder. Liesendahl would receive the same award, albeit posthumously.

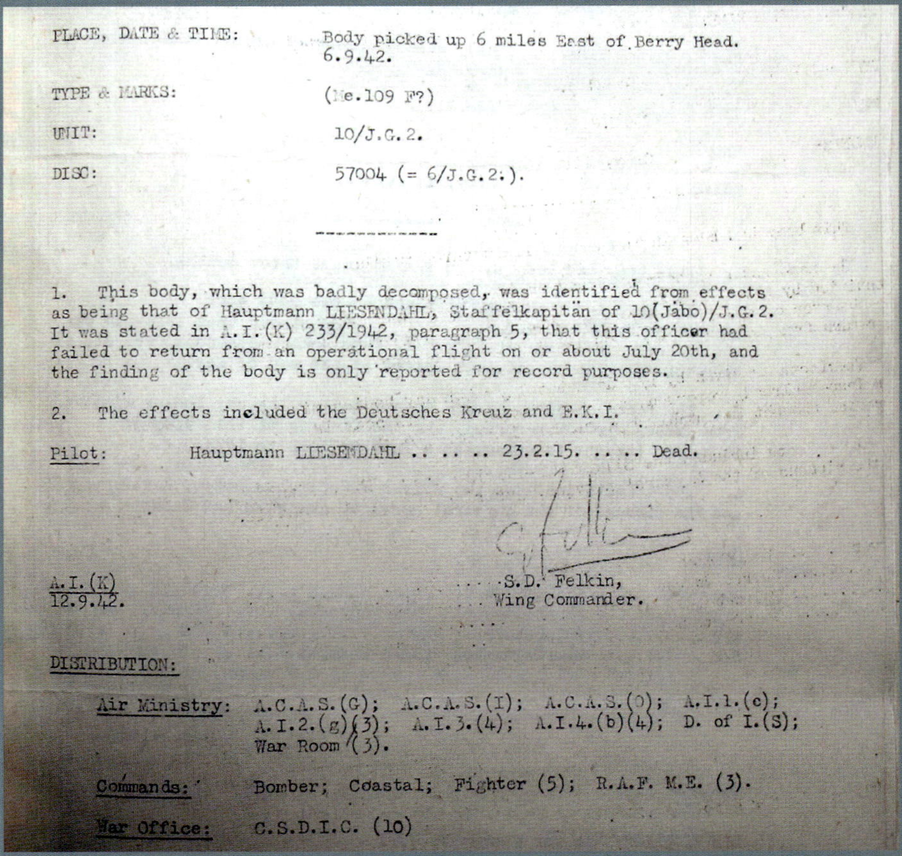

PLACE, DATE & TIME: Body picked up 6 miles East of Berry Head. 6.9.42.

TYPE & MARKS: (Me.109 F?)

UNIT: 10/J.G.2.

DISC: 57004 (= 6/J.G.2.).

----

1. This body, which was badly decomposed, was identified from effects as being that of Hauptmann LIESENDAHL, Staffelkapitän of 10(Jabo)/J.G.2. It was stated in A.I.(K) 233/1942, paragraph 5, that this officer had failed to return from an operational flight on or about July 20th, and the finding of the body is only reported for record purposes.

2. The effects included the Deutsches Kreuz and E.K.I.

Pilot: Hauptmann LIESENDAHL .. .. .. 23.2.15. .. .. Dead.

A.I.(K)
12.9.42.

S.D. Felkin,
Wing Commander.

DISTRIBUTION:

Air Ministry: A.C.A.S.(G); A.C.A.S.(I); A.C.A.S.(O); A.I.1.(c); A.I.2.(g)(3); A.I.3.(4); A.I.4.(b)(4); D. of I.(S); War Room (3).

Commands: Bomber; Coastal; Fighter (5); R.A.F. M.E. (3).

War Office: C.S.D.I.C. (10)

A British intelligence report on the discovery and return to the sea of the body of Hptm. Liesendahl.

3 Day Fighter Aces: Far North

The Far North theater was as vast as it was forbidding. From the Norwegian fjords to the Arctic wastes of northern Finland and the Barents Sea, through which Allied Artic convoys wound their way into the Soviet ports of Murmansk and Archangel, it was a challenging environment in which to conduct the business of war.

Although we are only studying the careers of three pilots in this theater, that does not diminish the importance the Luftwaffe allocated to this sector. The three aces are Karl-Heinz Koch (six kills), Felix-Maria Brandis (14 kills), and Heinrich Bartels with a staggering 97 victories (with a number of these attained in the Balkans and France).

Oberleutnant Felix-Maria Brandis

During Operation *Weserübung*, the invasion of Scandinavia, in April 1940, only one single-engine fighter unit (II./JG 77) was deployed. Given the large distances to be covered (especially in Norway), long-range, twin-engine Bf 110s were the primary fighter types deployed. The end of 1940 saw the Luftwaffe mainly concentrated in the West. But despite this shift in activity, operations continued in Northern Europe, with RAF Coastal Command aircraft regularly attacking German shipping supplying garrisons along the Norwegian coast. In early

January 1941 at Kristiansand-Kjevik, Lt. Felix-Maria Brandis, Ferry Laskovic, and Karl Fritz Schlossstein.

Bf 110C-4 “LN+HS” of Lt. Brandis on patrol over the snow-covered hills of Norway in late spring 1941.

January 1941, in order to beef up protection for the ships, eight *Zerstörer* crews, just out of training, arrived at Kjevik, Kristiansand's airfield, to form—somewhat haphazardly—the Jagdkommando Kjevik. The oldest officer, Lt. Felix Maria Brandis (born in Ahaus on September 9, 1916), was appointed temporary squadron leader (*Staffelführer*) before the unit was taken over by a more senior officer. But Brandis, given his seriousness and his competence, regularly led the unit in combat thereafter. The primary missions were patrolling and escorting ships.

On January 27, 1941, one of these flights almost proved fatal for Brandis and his partner, Gefr. Matthias Gans. Victims of an engine failure—the Bf 110s seem to have been old aircraft given up by other units—they were forced to ditch and only escaped death in the icy waters thanks to a Norwegian trawler which rescued them. Brandis recovered easily from this unfortunate episode as he shot down three Coastal Command twin-engine planes in April and June.

Nose armament and the badge adopted after *Barbarossa*: a dachshund holding an I-16 fighter in its mouth.

The launching of Operation *Barbarossa*, the invasion of the USSR on June 22, 1941, changed the fate of the squadron, which was eventually renamed 1.(Z)/JG 77 after several false starts, which made it part of the 77th Fighter Wing equipped with Bf 109s and not *Zerstörer* (the "Z" in its designation). It now had to deal directly with the Soviet Air Force around Murmansk. The Bf 110s operated from the Finnish airfields of Kirkenes and Petsamo. On June 27, 1941, Brandis's aircraft collided with another twin-engine aircraft of the unit, but both crews escaped without too much harm. On July 17, Brandis again came down at sea when his new aircraft (Bf 110D-3 W.Nr. 3710 "LN+AR") was hit by flak. He was unharmed but this time lost the radio gunner Matthias Gans who was reported missing.

Kapitän of the Dackelstaffel with the three mascots of 1.(Z)/JG 77: Herdla, Lockheed, and Bamse.

On September 1,1941, Brandis landed his aircraft in neutral Sweden after getting lost.

His Bf 110E-1 “LN+FR” was extensively photographed by the Swedish military.

During July 1941, Brandis was credited with three Soviet aircraft and two British Fleet Air Arm carrierborne Albacores attacking Kirkenes. On August 16, he scored his ninth victory over a Soviet fighter.

On September 1, 1941, lost with another Bf 110 in thick fog, Brandis landed at Tarando in Sweden. Although both aircraft were intact, their crews were interned. However, as the Swedish government looked favorably on the Reich (a state of affairs which would change in 1944), the four airmen stayed only a week in this neutral country before being sent back to Finland at the controls of their twin-engine planes.

On September 15, an I-16 piloted by Lt A. P. Olesov of 145 IAP was added to Brandis's scoreboard, but he had to crash-land the following day after the port engine of his Bf 110D-2 W.Nr. 3170 "LN+HR" was hit by several rounds of flak. A frantic search began with all available means. Finally, Brandis and his passenger Uffz. Guntram Weigl, an army observer, were recovered from no man's land. The ace won four more victories in October and November 1941.

By January 1942, Oblt. Brandis was officially *Kapitän* of 6.(Z)/JG 5, the new designation of the *Staffel*. On February 2, 1942, returning from leave, the commander was killed at the controls of Bf 110E-2 W.Nr. 2546 "LN+AR" when he hit the ground in bad weather near Pyavsero, after a mission to attack a railway convoy. His radio operator, Fw. Herbert Baus, although seriously wounded, survived. Brandis, credited with 14 victories, is now buried in the German military cemetery in Rovaniemi, Finland.

Although of indifferent quality, the 14 victory bars achieved by Brandis and his crew are clearly visible.

Brandis's victories

No	Date	Time	Aircraft	Unit	Place
1	Apr 9, 1941		Blenheim N3609 QY-H	254 Sqn	100km SW of Herdla
2	Apr 15, 1941	1512	Blenheim IV L8840 QY-P	254 Sqn	25mi SW of Bergen
3	Jun 1, 1941	1158	Hudson T9936 NR-R	220 Sqn	Bergen
4	Jul 21, 1941	1430	SB-3		Murmansk sector
5	Jul 22, 1941		I-18		Murmansk sector
6	Jul 25, 1941		I-16		Niva river
7	Jul 30, 1941		Albacore	827 or 828 Sqn RNAS	Kirkenes
8	Jul 30, 1941		Albacore	827 or 828 Sqn RNAS	Kirkenes
9	Aug 16, 1941		I-180		S of Taibola
10	Sep 15, 1941		I-16	145 IAP VVS	Murmansk sector
11	Oct, 24, 1941	1230	I-153	145 IAP VVS	Litsa/Oura-Gouba
12		1230	I-16	145 IAP VVS	
13	Oct, 25, 1941	1500	Hurricane		Murmansk sector
14	Nov 29, 1941	1300	I-18		Murmansk

Oberfeldwebel Heinrich Bartels

Heinrich Bartels was born in Linz (Austria) on July 13, 1918. His country being annexed during the Anschluss of 1938, he joined the Luftwaffe the following year. After his training, he was assigned in June 1941 to the Ergänzungsstaffel JG 26, an operational training unit, based in Wevelgem (Belgium) to be close to the 26th Wing. He was credited with two Spitfires in August during the RAF's "Non-Stop Offensive," the second of which

Rare colour view of Bf 109E "White 12" of 1. Erg/JG 26, Bartels' *Staffel*, at Rotterdam-Waalhaven in early summer 1941.

Petsamo, September 10, 1942: Uffz. Bartels returning from his 100th combat sortie is warmly welcomed by the his comrades in 8./JG 5. His Bf 109F-4 W.Nr. 13169 “Black 13,” christened “Hella,” bears the emblems of III./JG 5 and 8./JG 5.

was probably Mk IIA P8726 of No. 403 Squadron of the Royal Canadian Air Force (RCAF). When the Erg. St./JG 26 was redesignated 11./JG 1 at Vannes in early 1942, the young Austrian remained in this squadron which, in March 1942, became 8./JG 5 before deploying to Northern Europe to fight with the other elements of the Eismeergeschwader (the Arctic Sea Wing).

Uffz. Bartels quickly made his mark downing 44 Soviet aircraft up to November 13, 1942, when he was awarded the Knight's Cross. It is probable that this record is somewhat "inflated"—JG 5 regularly operated over enemy territory, in the Murmansk region, where it was impossible to examine wrecks that would confirm or deny these claims. A case in point are the six Hurricanes claimed shot down on September 22, at a time when "Stalin's Falcons" were no longer the "fat pigeons" of the early months of the campaign in the East. Nonetheless, Bartels seems to have been greatly appreciated by the other pilots. He was a swashbuckler, a dogfighting "specialist," and an excellent comrade who was always ready to assist his fellow pilots and give them any advice they needed to survive the tough battles of the Far North.

Uffz. Bartels took a leave of absence before achieving his last three victories over the Soviet Air Force on March 23, 1943. It was then that the Austrian's career took an astonishing turn. He left the cold wilderness of the Arctic tundras for the heavy Mediterranean heat. He was moved to 11./JG 27—part of IV Gruppe—which had just been formed at Kalamaki airfield near Athens. This transfer is surprising at first sight but a persistent rumor suggests that the pilot had accumulated debts, probably from gambling, and that he had narrowly escaped court martial. This also explains his retention of the rank of non-commissioned officer. After receiving the Knight's Cross, he should at least have been promoted to *Tapferkeitsoffizier* (officer by courage) like Walter Schuck or Johann Pichler. But the high command must have considered that a serious debt was an obstacle to any promotion, even as an exception.

Despite this sudden change of front, Fw. Bartels was to work hard as he had done in the North. And there was no shortage of opportunities when British forces tried to occupy the Dodecanese islands, after the Italian capitulation of September 8, 1943. Again, however, there were some exaggerated claims. For example, the two Bostons shot down on October 1 near the island of Kos amounted to no more than a single damaged Baltimore of No. 203 Squadron (they were not credited), and there is no trace of the two P-38s of October 31 in the Allied archives. Nevertheless, Bartels claimed 24 more victories by the end of 1943.

Having received the Knight's Cross, Bartels poses with his *Feldmütze* (cap) to which he has attached an Edelweiss badge, the distinctive symbol of the *Gebirgsjäger* (mountain fighters) with whom JG 5 fought so fiercely in the Far North.

Two views of Bartels' "Gustav" coded "Red 13" in 11./JG 27 in October 1943, in flight and on the ground. The ace seems to have favored the number 13. This Bf 109G-6, W.Nr. 27169, is fitted with the R6 modification kit—two additional 20mm guns under the wings—and was named "*Marga*," after his wife.

Bartels in his Bf 109G-6 "Red 13" at Kalamaki.

With his comrades, he faced not only Royal Air Force aircraft, but also P-38s and B-24s of the USAAF, which came later to the aid of its British ally.

During late 1943/early 1944, IV./JG 27 shifted to the former Yugoslavia, then to Austria, with the mission of countering the U.S. Fifteenth Air Force bombers attacking Austria and southern Germany. Bartels was credited with nine more victories in these engagements. By mid-1944, the *Gruppe* was part of the *Reichsverteidigung*, the defense of the Reich, and Bartels scored three more official victories in the skies over Germany. However, at that time, the Normandy landings were taking place (June 6 onward) and IV./JG 27 was among the *Gruppen* hastily sent to France. Operating from Champfleury, Bartels added 11 victories to his record in June. These successes led to his nomination for the Oak Leaves.

The withdrawal was rapid and, in the face of Allied numerical superiority, IV./JG 27 returned to German territory. Based in Achmer, Ofw. Bartels returned another victory in early December before being deployed with his comrades in Operation *Wacht am Rhein*, the battle of the Bulge. His 96th

Messerschmitt Bf 109G-6/R6 Trop W.Nr. 27169 "Red 13" *Marga* of Fw. Heinrich Bartels, 11./JG 27, Kalamaki, November 1943. Bartels is wearing his life jacket.

confirmed victory was achieved over the Eifel on December 18. On December 23, 1944, he took off from Achmer to counter a compact American formation over the Rhine. He shot down a P-47 of the 56th FG before his Bf 109G-10 W.Nr. 130359 "Yellow 13" was hit by fire from the "Wolf Pack" (nickname of the 56th Fighter Group). The Austrian pilot was reported missing. It was not until January 26, 1968, that his body was exhumed during a spot search along with the remains of his aircraft that had come down more than 20 years earlier in a field in Villip near Bad Godesberg. Obfw. Heinrich Bartels was subsequently buried in the local cemetery where he still lies. He flew at least 500 combat sorties.

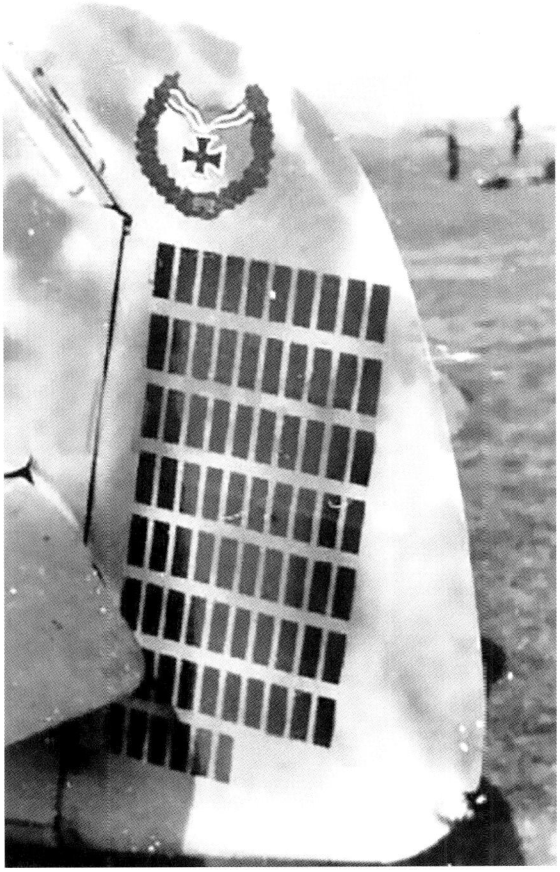

The rudder of his Bartles' new "Gustav" in April 1944 at Götzendorf, decorated with 76 victory bars and the Knight's Cross.

Bartels's victories

No	Date	Time	Aircraft	Unit	Place
1	Aug 19, 1941		Spitfire		Belgian/French border
2	Aug 27, 1941	1145	Spitfire		Wedumer/Alten
3	Apr 26, 1942	0950	Hurricane	769 IAP	Ura-Guba
4	May 10, 1942	1712	Hurricane	Northern Fleet	Motosvki
5	May 14, 1942	1835	I-16		Titovka
6	May 15, 1942	1815	Hurricane		Ura-Guba
7	May 17, 1942	0542	Hurricane		W Murmansk
8	May 19, 1942	0930	MiG-3		Litsa
9	Jul 29, 1942	1015	MiG-3		N Murmansk
10		1016	MiG-3		
11	Aug 5, 1942	1240	P-40		S Schongui
12		1245	P-40		S Mourmaschi
13	Aug 10, 1942	1850–1905	Hurricane	760 IAP	Ura-Guba
14			Hurricane	760 IAP	
15			Hurricane	760 IAP	
16	Aug 11, 1942	2020	Hurricane	197 IAP	Murmansk area
17	Aug 13, 1942	1500–1520	I-152		Murmansk area
18			P-40		
19			P-40		
20	Sep 2, 1942	1115	Airacobra		Kola
21		1120	Yak-7		Murmansk area
22		1125	P-40		
23	Sep 5, 1942	0825–0840	Hurricane		Murmansk/Kola
24			MiG-3		
25			MiG-3		
26	Sep 8, 1942	1135	Airacobra		Murmansk area
27		1508	P-40		
28		1509	P-40		
29	Sep 9, 1942	1035	Airacobra		Kola
30	Sep 11, 1942	1630–1537	Yak-7		N Murmansk
31			MiG-3		
32			MiG-3		

33	Sep 22, 1942	1207–1215	Hurricane		E Murmansk
34			Hurricane		
35			Hurricane		
36			Hurricane		
37		1530–1537	MiG-3		N Murmansk
38			MiG-3		
39	Sep 29, 1942	1255	Yak-7		E Murmansk
40		1256	Yak-7		
41	Oct 21, 1942	1325	MiG-3		Murmansk-Murmachi
42		1328	MiG-3		
43	Oct 29, 1942	1345–1356	LaGG-3	255e IAP	Murmansk area
44			LaGG-3	255e IAP	
45			LaGG-3	255e IAP	
46	Nov 5, 1942	1055	LaGG-3	255e IAP	Murmansk area
47	Mar 3, 1943	1415–1420	P-39		Pl. Qu. 36/2927
48			P-40		Pl. Qu. 36/3915
49			P-40		Pl. Qu. 36/2925
-	Oct 1, 1943		Boston B-26		NE Kos
-			Boston B-26		
50	Oct 5, 1943	1223	B-24D	376 BG	Petromogula/Márikon
51		1233	B-24D	376 BG	Petrálona
52	Oct 8, 1943	1315–1355	P-38	82 FG	S Leváhdia
53			P-38	82 FG	SW Cape of Kamena Vourla
54			P-38	82 FG	W Velanidia
55	Oct 23, 1943	1311	Spitfire	208a Squadron	SW Podgorica
56	Oct 25, 1943	1316–1322	P-38		N Cape Rodon
57			Whitley/B-25		S Bar
58			P-38		S Bar
59			P-38		N Cape Rodon
60	Oct 31, 1943	1515	P-38		Cape Rodon
61		1520	P-38		
62	Nov 2, 1943	1347	Spitfire		SE Scutari
63			Spitfire		

64	Nov 4, 1943	1625	Boston B-26	14 Squadron	W Durazzo
65	Nov 15, 1943	1310–1312	P-38		SE Kalamaki
66			P-38		
67			P-38		
68			P-38		
69	Nov 17, 1943	1250	B-25	486 FG	NE Kalamaki
70		1252	B-25	340 FG	
71		1258	P-38		E Marathon
72	Apr 11, 1944	1632	P-38		NW Graz
73	Apr 23, 1944	0820–0823	Spitfire		SW Celje
74			Spitfire		
75			Spitfire		
76	Apr 24, 1944	1345	P-51	357/355 FG	W Mühldorf
77	Apr 24, 1944	1347	P-51		W Mühldorf
78		1347	P-51		N Waldkraiburg
79	Apr 28, 1944	1038	P-51	352 FG	NE Laibach (Ljubjana)
80		1039	P-51	503 FS/339 FG	
81	May 19, 1944	1325–1330	P-47		Quedlinburg
82			P-47		
83			P-51		
84	Jun 14, 1944	0728–0730	P-47	377 FS/362 FG	Falaise/Argentan
85			P-47	377 FS/362 FG	
86			P-47	377 FS/362 FG	
87		0805	P-47		SW Paris
88	Jun 16, 1944	2047	P-47		Dives-sur-Mer
89		2048	P-47		
90	Jun 22, 1944	1410	Spitfire		SE Caen
91		1417	P-51		Evrecy
92	Jun 24, 1944	1505	P-51		Flers
93		1508	P-51		
94	Jun 25, 1944	0905	P-38		SE Blois
95	Dec 8, 1944	0950	P-51		NW Achmer
96	Dec 18, 1944	1348	P-51		Eifer
97	Dec 23, 1944		P-47	56 FG	nr Bad Godesberg

Oberleutnant Karl-Heinz Koch

Born on December 16, 1919 in Hildesheim, Karl-Heinz "Charly" Koch, after his pilot training with 2./JG 102 and 4./JG Ost, was transferred in July 1943 to 4./JG 3 which operated on the Eastern Front. He remained there for a short time because, in early August, II./JG 3 returned to the West to be engaged in the defense of the Reich, being based first at Ütersen and then at Schiphol. On September 22, Lt. Koch was credited with his first victory, over a P-47 but, with his engine hit, he had to make an emergency landing in his Bf 109G-6 W.Nr. 15628 "White 5." On three separate occasions the following month—October 11, 15, and 20, 1943—he was again forced to make an emergency landing after a fight, on the last occasion in Bf 109G-6 W.Nr. 20067 "White 8." On March 8, 1944, while operating out of Gardelegen, he obtained a *Herausschuss* of a B-24, damaging it and forcing it out of formation, making it more vulnerable. TO of II./JG 3, he is also mentioned as having led 4. Staffel. However, there is no official record of this, but it is very likely that, by virtue of his rank, Lt. Koch did indeed temporarily command his *Staffel* (as *Staffelführer*) in the absence of the acting *Staffelkapitän*.

At the end of May 1944, Oblt. Koch was transferred to 11./JG 5 in the North: according to his own account, he was ashamed of the fact that he had been forced to make several crash landings during the fighting over Germany. Together with the *Eismeergeschwader* ace, Lt. Walter Schuck, he shot down a Yak-9 on September 27, 1944. On October 9, he was credited with an Il-2 and on October 23, with a Boston. He then alternated between *Staffeln* of the *Eismeergeschwader*—14./JG 5,and 13./JG 5—before leading 12./JG 5 in February 1945. He ended the war at the head of 5./JG 5 (new designation of 12./JG 5), making his last flight on April 7, 1945 from Herdla. Karl-Heinz Koch died in Dassel on March 10, 2001.

Lt. "Charly" Koch at Herdla at the end of 1944.

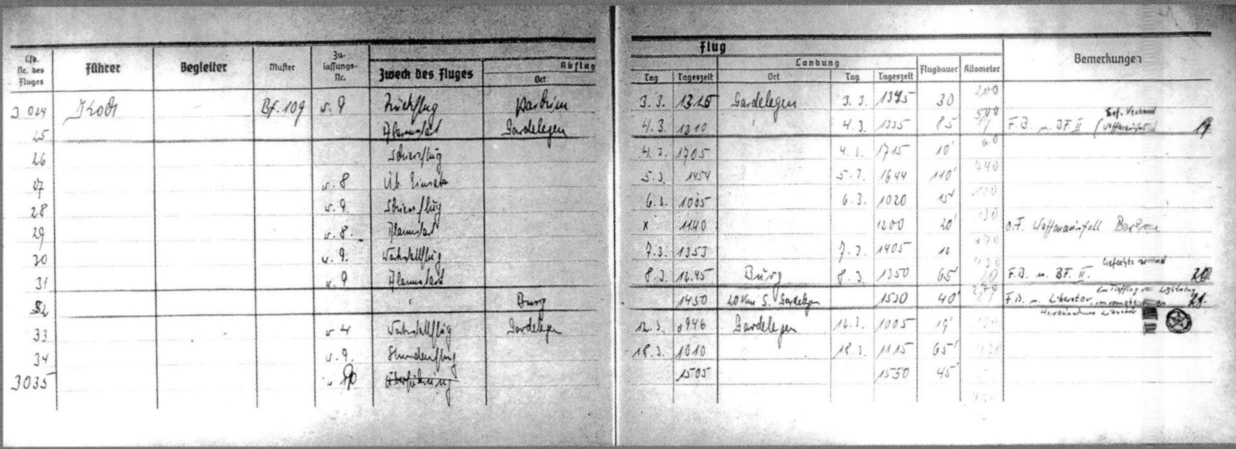

Lfd. Nr. des Fluges	Führer	Begleiter	Muster	Zulassungs-Nr.	Zweck des Fluges	Abflug Ort	Abflug Tag	Abflug Tageszeit	Landung Ort	Landung Tag	Landung Tageszeit	Flugdauer	Kilometer	Bemerkungen
3 024	Koch	–	Bf. 109	v. 9	[illegible]	[illegible]	3. 3.	1315	Gardelegen	3. 3.	1345	30	200	
25					Alarmstart	Gardelegen	4. 3.	1210		4. 3.	1335	85	500	F.B. m. BF. II [illegible] 19
26					[illegible]		4. 3.	1705		4. 3.	1715	10'	60	
27				v. 8	Üb. Einsatz		5. 3.	1454		5. 3.	1644	110'	740	
28				v. 9	[illegible]		6. 3.	1005		6. 3.	1020	15'	[illegible]	
29				v. 8.	Alarmstart		x	1140			1200	20'	[illegible]	O.F. Waffenausfall [illegible]
30				v. 9.	Werkstattflug		7. 3.	1353		7. 3.	1405	12	[illegible]	
31				v. 9	Alarmstart		8. 3.	12.45	Burg	8. 3.	1350	65'	[illegible]	F.B. m. BF. II. [illegible] 20
32						Burg		1450	20 km S. Gardelegen		1530	40'	270	F.B. m. Liberator [illegible] 21
33				v. 4	Werkstattflug	Gardelegen	12. 3.	0946	Gardelegen	12. 3.	1005	19'		
34				v. 9.	[illegible]		18. 3.	1010		18. 3.	1115	65'		
3035				v. 10	Überführung			1505			1550	45'		

An extract from Koch's *Flugbuch* (logbook) with his second victory: the *Herrausschuss* of a B-24.

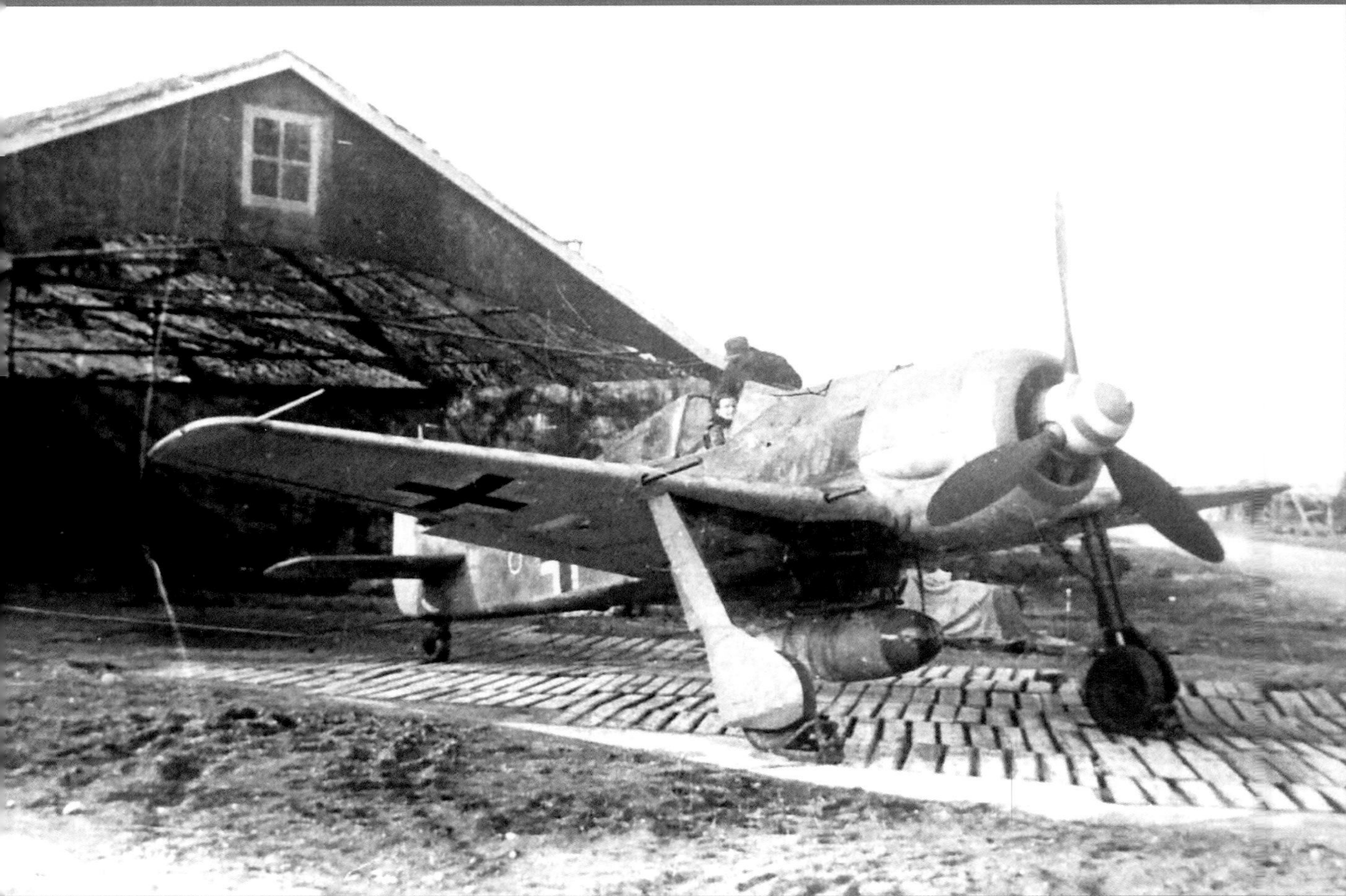

Lt. Koch in his Fw 190A-8 "Blue 9" at Herdla, early 1945.

Koch's victories

No	Date	Time	Aircraft	Unit	Place
1	Sep 22, 1943	1315	P-47		SW of Utrecht
2	Mar 8, 1944	1100	B-24 HSS		Gardelegen sector
3	Sep 27, 1944	1140	Yak-9		vicinity of Murmansk
4	Oct 9, 1944	1515	Il-2		Pechenga
5	Oct 23, 1944	0950	Boston		Pechenga
6	Feb 9, 1945	1612	P-51		Fjord Førde

Staka Koch's Fw 190 with five victory marks on its tailfin.

4

Day Fighter Aces: North Africa and the Mediterranean

This theater was as diverse as it was large, stretching from Gibraltar in the west to the Levant in the east, and from the Italian Alps and the Balkans in the north, south across the Mediterranean with its plethora of island campaigns—Crete, Malta, Sicily—to the Western Desert of North Africa. It was here that the Wehrmacht would come up against the Americans for the first time, during Operation *Torch*.

We focus on two Luftwaffe aces in this chapter: Fritz Dinger with 67 victories—a few from Stalingrad, but the bulk from combat in the Mediterranean and in particular against Spitfires and Hurricanes in the skies over Malta; and Heinz-Arnold Stahlschmidt, the second pilot, with 59 victories, mainly won over the skies of the Western Desert, particularly around El Alamein.

Oberleutnant Fritz Dinger

Born on August 20, 1915, in Ottweiler, Saarland, Friedrich "Fritz" Dinger was a reserve pilot in the Lufwaffe. In August 1939, as war threatened, the young *Feldwebel* was called up to 4./JG 53. He took part in the offensive in the West but did not manage any victories. On August 16, 1940, Dinger's Bf 109E-1 was shot down in combat in the English Channel. Slightly wounded, the pilot was rescued by the Seenot (search and rescue) near Cherbourg. At the end of 1940, he was promoted to *Leutnant*.

Staffelkapitän of 4./JG 53, Fritz Dinger and his mascot "Hella."

October 5, 1941, Lt. Dinger crash-landed his Bf 109F-4 after being hit by Soviet flak. The rudder shows his first 10 victories in the East.

However, he had to wait a year, for the opening of the Eastern Front before he could score any victories. On 1 July, he earned his first two victories over Soviet aircraft. Eight other *Luftsiege* followed during the summer. On October 5, 1941, victim of flak fire at Sologoubovka, 70 kilometers southeast of Leningrad, Lt. Dinger placed his Bf 109F-4 "White 4" (W.Nr. 7187) on its belly in an emergency landing. The fighter ended up on the side of a road, but the pilot was unharmed.

Shortly afterwards, II./JG 53 returned to the West after weeks of hard work in the USSR. The *Gruppe*, based in the Netherlands, fought mainly RAF light bombers. On October 27, Dinger was credited with a Blenheim from No 114 Squadron (his 11th victory) near the island of Texel.

By this time, the war had gained momentum in the Mediterranean, with the island of Malta becoming a formidable thorn in the side of the Axis forces. II./JG 53 was to undergo a new change of front, the unit reaching Sicily to operate in the skies over Malta. On the morning of February 22, 1942, Lt. Dinger was credited with a Hurricane, which could not be confirmed (as would be the case for many claims over Malta, as the situation there was so confused).

Dinger stayed in Sicily for a few weeks, adding a Hurricane and four Spitfires to his record of achievement during these exhausting and hotly contested battles. At the end of July, he was seconded to the Stab I/JG 53 to reinforce this *Gruppe*, which was then engaged in the USSR in the Stalingrad sector. Several authors have underlined the astonishing laxity of the local authorities in charge of compiling

or forwarding the claims on this part of the front. This is how I./JG 53, having converted onto the Bf 109G-2, amassed an astonishing number of victories. Dinger took advantage of this "Soviet windfall"—as did everyone else. Having left the Mediterranean with 18 victories, he returned in October credited with … 48 *Abschüsse*! As losses over Malta had been significant, Dinger, given his undeniable experience, was promoted to *Oberleutnant* upon his return to Sicily, a rank that allowed him to lead 4./JG 53.

Even though his "score" had been somewhat "boosted" in the East, Dinger once again demonstrated his qualities as a fighter pilot by downing a Spitfire over Malta. However, in Libya, the Afrikakorps was in retreat and II./JG 53 was forced to fall back into Tunisia to support the disparate

Abandoned on the spot, this aircraft was frequently photographed by passing infantrymen.

Sicily 1942. 4./JG 53 celebrates Fritz Dinger's 400th combat sortie. He flew more than 600 up to his death.

Axis forces surrounded on all sides. On December 5, 1942, the *Staka* of 4./JG 53 shot down his first American twin-engine bomber and, on December 23, he was awarded the Knight's Cross for 49 victories (he was already at 53 by this date). He was then temporarily withdrawn from the front and took advantage of this well-deserved leave to get married.

By May 1943, Africa had been evacuated and II./JG 53 had fallen back on Sicily to continue the fight. The ace had returned four new victories in April as his *Gruppe* faced overwhelming Allied superiority. On July 20, Dinger had to withdraw with his men to the Italian mainland, to the airfield of Scalea. During Operation *Husky*, the Allied landings on Sicily, he nevertheless won seven victories. But on Tuesday July 27, 1943, after having disposed of an A-36 Invader fighter-bomber (s/n 42-84059 of

Eastern Front, September 1942. Mechanics update Dinger's record on the rudder of his Bf 109G-2.

Dinger speaking to the mechanics and armorers of 4. Staffel in Tunisia, early 1943.

the 16th BS/27th FBG), his 67th claim, two waves of bombers escorted by P-38s appeared over Scalea. Running to his Bf 109G for an *Alarmstart* (emergency scramble), Dinger was hit in the neck by a bomb splinter and killed instantly. Much appreciated by his men, a "joker" and a "go-getter," Oblt. Fritz Dinger was buried the next day on the site, along with three mechanics who were also victims of the lightning attack. He is buried today in the large German cemetery at Monte Cassino.

The commander of 4./JG 53 lights up in front of the rudder of his Bf 109G-4. His record was 53 victories.

Dinger's victories

No	Date	Time	Aircraft	Unit	Place
1	Jul 4, 1941	1646	SB-3	41 BAD	Daugavpils
2		1647	SB-3	41 BAD	
3		1648	SB-3	41 BAD	
4	Jul 10, 1941	0903	SB-3	41 BAD	
5	Jul 11, 1941		SB-3	41 BAD	
6	Aug 25, 1941	1342	I-18 (MiG-1)		
7	Aug 29, 1941	1527	I-16		
8		1622	V-11 (Il-2)		
9		1846	I-16		
10	Sep 28, 1941	1609	Pe-2		Leningrad area
11	Oct 27, 1941	1508	Blenheim IV V5888 or Z7309	114 Sqn	6km NW Texel
12	Feb 22, 1942	1205	Hurricane		Malta
13	Apr 22, 1942	1030	Hurricane		Malta
14	Jun 15, 1942	1825	Spitfire		50 km SW Gozo
15	Jul 2, 1942	0748	Spitfire		15km NE La Valette
16	Jul 7, 1942	0656	Spitfire		Malta
17	Jul 10, 1942	1041	Spitfire		Malta
18	Jul 13, 1942	1330	Spitfire		5–10km S Kalafrana
19	Aug 18, 1942	1723	Il-2		W Chintov
20	Aug 19, 1942	1130	Pe-2		E Kousserov
21		1131	LaGG-3		
22		1747	Il-2		25km NW Gumrak
23	Aug 21, 1942	1730	LaGG-3		35km NW Gumrak
24	Aug 25, 1942	1106	MiG-1		25km NE Stalingrad
25	Aug 30, 1942	0811	I-180 (Yak-7)		30km S Stalingrad
26		0858	Il-2		Grebenka area
27		0900	Il-2		
28	Aug 31, 1942	0900	Il-2		30km SE Stalingrad
29	Sep 3, 1942	0943	Il-2	289 SAD	25km E Stalingrad
30		1510	Yak-1		40km N Gumrak
31	Sep 6, 1942	1015	LaGG-3		55km E Stalingrad
32	Sep 7, 1942	1124	Il-2		30km N Gumrak
33		1554	Il-2		

Dinger's return from combat at the controls of Bf 109G-4 Trop "White 4" at La Marsa airfield, March 1943. The local population, quite favorable to the Germans, showed great admiration for the Luftwaffe.

With his men of 4. Staffel at La Marsa, near Tunis, in March 1943. Dinger seems to have been a valued leader and a loyal comrade.

34	Sep 10, 1942	1403	LaGG-3		20km SE Stalingrad
35	Sep 11, 1942	1443	Yak-1		5km NE Kotluban
36	Sep 13, 1942	0640	I-180 (Yak-7)		35km E Stalingrad
37		0658	I-180 (Yak-7)		10km E Stalingrad
38	Sep 15, 1942	0936	Il-2		NE Stalingrad
39		0937	Il-2		
40	Sep 16, 1942	0940	La-5		SE Stalingrad
41	Sep 19, 1942		Il-2	289 SAD	Stalingrad area
42			Il-2	289 SAD	
43	Sep 23, 1942	0640	La-5		N Grebenka
44		1640	Yak-1		NE Grebenka
45	Sep 24, 1942	0706	MiG-1		30km N Gumrak
46	Sep 25, 1942	1048	MiG-1		N Stalingrad
47		1052	Il-2		
48		1632	Yak-1		75km NNE Stalingrad
49	Oct 16, 1942	0825	Spitfire		3–5km E Zukor
50	Dec 4, 1942	1131	P-38F	1st FG	2km S Ferryville
51		1550	Boston Bisley?	18 or 614 Sqn	30km SE Mateur
52		1552	Boston Bisley?		
53	Dec 5, 1942	1231	B-25 (A-20)	310th BG	10km W Cap Blanc
54	Mar 22, 1943	1355	B-26	17th BG	E of Cani
55	Apr 5, 1943	0913	P-38F	82nd FG	40km N Zembra
56	Apr 18, 1943	1902	P-40	47th FG	10km SW Ras el Amas
57	Apr 19, 1943	1557	Spitfire V	417 Sqn	10km W Zembra
58	Apr 25, 1943	1359	Spitfire V	31st FG	10km S Hammamet
59	Jun 4, 1943	0756	Spitfire IX EN532	126 Sqn	20km N La Valette
60	Jul 6, 1943	1522	Spitfire	308th FS/31st FG	1km W Pozzalo
61	Jul 7, 1943	1718	P-40		35km SW Marsalla
62	Jul 8, 1943	1225	B-17		20km S Agrigento
63		1618	P-40L	315th FS/324th FG	W Sciacca
64	Jul 9, 1943	0743	P-40	316th FS/324th FG	2–3km NNE Sciacca
65	Jul 18, 1943	0745	Spitfire		Catania
66	Jul 24, 1943	1255	B-26	320th BG	30km NE Stromboli
67	Jul 27, 1943		P-40 (A-36)	16th BS/27th FBG	

Lt. Heinz-Arnold Stahlschmidt photographed on the occasion of his commissioning in late 1940.

Oberleutnant Heinz-Arnold Stahlschmidt

Heinz-Arnold was born on September 5, 1920 in Kreuztal, the eldest son of an entrepreneur. After his time at the Reichsarbeitsdienst (Labour Office), he applied for the Luftwaffe. Transferred to 2./JG 27 in January 1941, he and his unit carried out a few brief operations in March over Malta from Sicily before leading a handful of missions over northern Yugoslavia during Operation *Marita*, the invasion of the Balkans, in April. On April 17, he left Europe for Castel Benito, Benghazi airport, I./JG 27 being the first single-engine fighter unit to arrive in support of the Afrikakorps. Numerous free-hunt, escort, reconnaissance, and ground strafing sorties followed. During quieter periods, bored young pilots looked to other less-conventional operations. Researchers Shores and Ring cite the anecdote of the "Battle of the Gulf of Bomba" (northeastern Libya), in which a *Schwarm* from 2./JG 27 flew over the sea at low altitude to strafe a small 200-ton Allied freighter before setting it on fire. The captain and crew managed to evacuate the ship and were captured. This "victory" was attributed to Ofhr. (officer candidate) Heinz-Arnold Stahlschmidt, who was ribbed by his comrades who accused him of having simply knocked over the crew's oil lamps.

On June 15, during Operation *Battleaxe*, Ofhr. Stahlschmidt won his first aerial victory over a Hawker Hurricane of No. 73 Squadron. He had to wait for the British *Crusader* offensive in order to achieve success in dramatic fashion, shooting down three No. 21 Squadron Martin 167 Maryland aircraft on November 20, 1941. "Fiffi," labeled a joker, formed a friendship with the future great ace Hans-Joachim Marseille, the other joker in the *Gruppe*.

Deployed as cover on February 21, 1942, Stahlschmidt was surprised by Curtiss P-40s of No. 112 Squadron. However, he managed to keep his Bf 109F-4 Trop W.Nr. 8528 in the air until he reached no man's land where he made an emergency landing. Slightly injured, he extricated himself from his burning machine and then crossed a minefield. Back in Martuba, he learnt that the commander had prematurely declared him killed in action. The decidedly unlucky young pilot had another misadventure five days later when his engine failed, and he had to make another emergency landing—on this occasion in the middle of a concentration of Allied vehicles near Ain-el-Gazala. Pulled from his cockpit by excited Polish soldiers, he was maltreated, and his decorations stolen. Refusing to speak during a strenuous interrogation, he was sequestered in a tent but, despite two broken

Mechanics of 2./JG 27 seen playing a game of Skat (a popular German card game) on the Libyan field of Ain-el-Gazala in late spring 1941. Heinz-Arnold had been a member of this *Staffel* since January. Bf 109E-7 Trop "Black 3" serves as a colorful backdrop with its "zebra-striped" camouflage retained from its previous owner, I./JG 3.

"Fiffi" Stahlschmidt in discussion with another great "African" ace, Lt. Werner Schroer (61 victories in this theater) in late 1941/early 1942, with Bf 109F-4 Trop "Red 5" in the background.

Airmen of JG 27 pictured here in front of a Bf 109F-4 Trop of I. Gruppe. There are six black victory bars on the rudder, a figure reached by "Fiffi" on December 14, 1941. He had recently been appointed adjutant of I./JG 27.

ribs and a fracture, Stahlschmidt evaded his sleepy guards and walked 80 kilometers back to his lines. On March 2, he was sent home to recover from this misadventure.

Returning to Africa with a morale of steel, he continued to accumulate successes despite two further forced landings on May 7 and July 21. Promoted to *Staffelkapitän* of 2./JG 27 from July 1, Stahlschmidt was credited with 25 victories in four weeks. As a result, his name began to appear in the Afrikakorps communiqués. On the 20th, he received the Knight's Cross for 45 victories. The most violent clashes took place in September 1942 during Rommel's offensive against Alam el Halfa. On September 3, with his comrade Marseille, the *Staka* Sathlschmidt shot down no less than five aircraft. On September 5, he announced the destruction of a Spitfire and a P-40 and claimed another Curtiss P-40 for his 59th victory the next day.

If "Fiffi" had always done well until then, his lucky star abandoned him on September 7,

Promoted to *Staffelkapitän* of 2./JG 27 on July 1, 1942, Stahlschmidt, seen here in a "Friedrich" of 1. Staffel (white code), will be credited with 25 RAF aircraft during the month.

1942. During a *Freie Jagd*, his unit once again went into action against several Desert Air Force formations, 30 kilometers southeast of El Alamein. Although two members of the *Schwarm* managed to return to Quotaifiya and another Bf 109 landed in the German lines, the commander of 2./JG 27 was reported missing aboard Bf 109F-4 Trop W.Nr. 8704 "Red 4." The search would remain fruitless. According to several sources, he was shot

Heinz-Arnold Stahlschmidt poses at Quotaifya next to the rudder of his Bf 109F-4 Trop after his 48th victory claimed on August 23, 1942. Three days prior to this, the ace had been awarded the Knight's Cross. Also visible is the silhouette of the 200-ton freighter attributed to the ace during the "Battle of the Bomba Gulf" in early June 1941.

Stahlschmidt (left) and the great ace Hans-Joachim Marseille. Like his comrade, Heinz-Arnold would gain a reputation as a formidable fighter in the skies over Africa.

down by Flt Lt John H. "Crash" Curry (eight victories), an American pilot flying with No. 601 Squadron on Spitfires. The Oak Leaves would be awarded to him posthumously on January 3, 1944, as well as a promotion to the rank of *Oberleutnant*. Although the efforts of the propaganda services kept him in the shadow of Marseille, Heinz-Arnold Stahlschmidt was nevertheless able to accomplish more combat sorties (400) than his comrade from Berlin.

Lt. Stahlschmidt pictured with the Knight's Cross. Up to his death on September 7, 1942, he shot down 59 Allied aircraft in North Africa. He was the third most successful ace in this theater, behind Marseille and Schroer.

Stahlschmidt's victories

No	Date	Time	Aircraft	Unit	Place
1	Jun 15, 1941	1140	Hurricane	73 Sqn	Sollum
2	Nov 20, 1941	1220	Maryland	21 (SAAF) Sqn	SE Tobruk
3		1225	Maryland	21 (SAAF) Sqn	
4		1230	Maryland	21 (SAAF) Sqn	
5	Nov 27, 1941	1620	Hurricane		S El Adem
6	Dec 14, 1941	1120	P-40		S Tmimi
7	Jan 11, 1942	1248	P-40	3 (SAAF) Sqn	NE Agedabia
8	Jan 22, 1942	1250	P-40	3 (SAAF) Sqn	E Gtafia
9	May 22, 1942	0750	P-40	112 or 150 Sqn	SW Tmimi
10	May 29, 1942	0749	P-40	N Fort Acroma	450 Sqn
11	Jun 13, 1942	0652	Hurricane	213 Sqn	Tobruk
12	Jun 14, 1942	1108	P-40	5 (SAAF) Sqn	NNW Gambut
13	Jun 16, 1942	1525	P-40		SW Gambut
14	Jun 26, 1942	1220	Hurricane	112 Sqn	nr Marsa Matruh
15		1225	Hurricane	112 Sqn	
16		1230	P-40	112 Sqn	
17		1906	P-40	260 Sqn	
18	Jun 27, 1942	1305	P-40	260 Sqn	SE Fuka
19	Jul 2, 1942	0625	Beaufighter	252 Sqn	N Fuka
20		1823	P-40	2 (SAAF) Sqn	Burj al Arab
21	Jul 3, 1942	1509	Hurricane	213 Sqn	SE El Alamein
22		1515	Hurricane	213 Sqn	
23	Jul 4, 1942	0630	P-40	450 Sqn	El Alamein
24		0632	P-40	450 Sqn	
25		0825	Hurricane	213 Sqn	
26		1705	Hurricane	1 (SAAF) Sqn	SW Burj al Arab
27	Jul 7, 1942	0602	"Gladiator" (Albacore)	826 RNAS Sqn	NE El Daba
28	Jul 8, 1942	1032	Hurricane IIC	33 Sqn	El Alamein/Burj Al Arab
29		1037	Hurricane IIC	33 Sqn	
30		1040	Hurricane IIC	33 Sqn	

31	Jul 10, 1942	1325	Hurricane	80 or 127 Sqn	El Alamein
32		1330	Hurricane	80 or 127 Sqn	
33		1335	Hurricane	80 or 127 Sqn	
34	Jul 11, 1942	1610	P-40	2 or 5 (SAAF) Sqn	SW El Alamein
35	Jul 14, 1942	1829	Spitfire	601 Sqn	El Alamein
-	Jul 15, 1942		Hurricane	213 Sqn	W El Hammam
36	Jul 16, 1942	1015	Hurricane	127 Sqn	SE El Alamein
37	Jul 17, 1942	1325	Hurricane	92 or 238 Sqn	SW El Alamein
38	Jul 22, 1942	0825	P-40	112 Sqn	W El Alamein
39		0840	P-40	4 (SAAF) Sqn	SW El Alamein
40		1200	Hurricane	73 Sqn	S El Alamein
41	Jul 27, 1941	1226	Hurricane	33 or 213 Sqn	S El Hammam
42		1720	Hurricane	1 (SAAF) Sqn	SW El Alamein
43		1742	P-40	3 (SAAF) or 450 Sqn	W El Alamein
44	Aug 1, 1942	1640	Hurricane	80 Sqn	W El Alamein
45		1645	Hurricane	80 Sqn	
46	Aug 16, 1942	0815	P-40	5 (SAAF) Sqn	NW El Hammam
47		0825	P-40	5 (SAAF) Sqn	WSW El Alamein
48	Aug 23, 1942	0803	P-40	3 (SAAF) or 450 Sqn	S El Hammam
49	Sep 1, 1942	1748	Hurricane	213 Sqn	SE El Alamein
50		1750	Hurricane	213 Sqn	
51	Sep 2, 1942	1612	Hurricane	274 Sqn	SW El Hammam
52	Sep 3, 1942	0722	P-40	145 Sqn	SW El Hammam
53		0725	P-40	145 Sqn	
54		0729	Spitfire	145 Sqn	
55		1512	Hurricane	7 (SAAF) Sqn	SW El Imayid
56		1526	P-40	7 (SAAF) Sqn	
57	Sep 5, 1942	1049	P-40	145 Sqn	El Imayid
58		1052	Spitfire	145 Sqn	
59	Sep 6, 1942	1725	P-40	5 (SAAF) Sqn	El Hammam

5

Night Fighter Aces

Night fighters were a special breed of airmen who prowled the night skies over Germany, often alone and against vast odds, but always seeking out those "*Pulks*" of Allied bombers. Uniquely trained on instruments, most night fighter pilots had never intended their particular role, but through a series of circumstances, fearlessness, and skills, had almost "fallen into" night-fighting.

Selected in this chapter are four night-fighter aces who were involved in the defense of the Reich. Wolfgang Falck, with seven victories, is clearly regarded as the father of the *Nachtjagd* community.

Martin Drewes with 47 victories, Egmont zur Lippe-Weissenfeld with 49, and Ludwig Meister with 39 kills, are the other three aces who achieved such startling success against the never-ending waves of the Allied *Viermots*.

Oberst Wolfgang Falck

Despite achieving all his victories by day, Wolfgang "Wolf" Falck is considered to be one of the founding fathers of the Nachtjagd, the German night fighter arm. The son of a pastor, he was born on August 19, 1910 in Berlin, his family coming from the region of Graudenz (today in Poland). In April 1931, after passing his

Wolfgang Falck at the controls of his Bf 110C-1 "M8+GK," seen here probably during the Polish campaign in September 1939. The radio operator seated behind him is Uffz. Alfred Watz. The ladybird lucky charm emblem under the cockpit was selected by Falck for 2./ZG 76 and was a tribute to his father, a foot soldier during the Great War, who had carved a similar lucky charm during a stay in Lille.

April 9, 1940. A mischievous mechanic chalks in a seventh victory bar on the port tailfin of Wolfgang Falck's Bf 110. The *Kommandeur* of I./ZG 1 had shot down three Polish, three British, and one Danish aircraft.

Abitur (secondary school leaving certificate), he joined the 100,000-man Reichswehr. Selected, he was able to train at the Deutsche Verkehrsfliegerschule, the German Air Transport School, in Schleissheim and in the summer of 1932 he trained clandestinely on the Fokker D.XIII at Lipetzk, thanks to an agreement signed with the Soviets. After six months, he returned to Germany and was transferred to the infantry, where he had to work hard until March 1935 when he became an instructor at the Deutsche Verkehrsfliegerschule. On April 1, 1936, Falck was simultaneously promoted to the rank of *Oberleutnant* and transferred to 5. Staffel of the brand-new Jagdgeschwader 132 "Richthofen" based at Jüterbog-Damm. There he continued to train young pilots before taking charge of a *Staffel* in III. Gruppe from July 1, 1938.

Wolfgang Falck with the Knight's Cross awarded on October 1, 1940. He remained at the head of NJG 1, the 1st Night Fighter Wing, for three years.

Bf 110E-1 "G9+GA" assigned to Falck as *Kommodore* NJG 1 seen during February 1942 during the so-called "Channel Dash."

Shortly before the outbreak of hostilities, his *Gruppe* was redesignated I./ZG 76 and equipped with Bf 110s at the controls of which Falck returned three *Abschüsse* over Poland.

On December 17, 1939, I./ZG 76 was transferred to Jever, to protect the German Bight. The next day, Falck took part in the famous battles against the RAF, claiming two Blenheims shot down. He then took over I./ZG 1 and claimed his last *Luftsieg* over a Norwegian Fokker D.XXI. Falck had always been interested in night hunting and even attempted some interceptions in May/June from Scandinavia. He subsequently wrote up some of these sorties, which came to the attention of the Luftwaffe hierarchy. He was then appointed head of the Nacht und Versuchsstaffel (experimental night-hunting unit) before he took command of NJG 1 and developed the *Helle Nachtjagd* (illuminated night fighting procedure), organized around a close collaboration between detection centers, searchlights, and night fighters. His efforts were rewarded by the Knight's Cross on October 1, 1940. After three years at the head of NJG 1, he was transferred to the staff of Josef Kammhuber, the commander of the Nachtjagd, but disagreements led to his departure. Close to Göring, Falck established new services and in 1943 he found himself in Romania, charged with organizing an air defense system that was effective enough to be adopted by the new post-war communist government. Oberst

The *Kommodore* bids farewell to his dog before boarding Bf 110E-1 W.Nr. 3920 for a cover sortie over the German capital ships during February 1942. Note eight victory markings on the tailfin.

(since July 1, 1943) Falck would then coordinate the actions of night and day fighters in the defense of the Reich. After the attempt on Hitler's life, he left for Belgrade to command the Balkan fighter units. In October 1944, he joined the staff of General der Fliegerausbildung and in May 1945, he was captured in Bad Aibling. Released a month later, he worked in a variety of jobs and in the 1960s joined North American Aviation before working as a consultant for McDonnell Douglas until 1986. Retired in the Austrian Tyrol, the likeable Wolfgang "Wolf" Falck died on March 13, 2007.

At Deelen airfield, Werner Streib—in symbolic horseplay—removes Wolfgang Falck from the command of NJG 1 in front of Falck's Bf 110 displaying his ladybird emblem. Streib took over from his illustrious predecessor on July 1, 1943 and achieved 68 victories.

Falck's victories

No	Date	Time	Aircraft	Unit	Place
1	Sep 5, 1939		PZL 23		Dalikow
2	Sep 11, 1939		Fokker F.IX		nr Byalistok
3			unidentified		
4	Dec 18, 1939		Wellington		nr Helgoland
			Wellington		
5	Jan 10, 1940		Blenheim	110 Sqn	North Sea
6	Feb 17, 1940		Blenheim	110 Sqn	N Ameland
7	Apr 9, 1940		Fokker D.XXI		Vaerlöse

Major Martin Drewes

Son of a pharmacist, Martin Drewes was born on October 20, 1918, in Lobmachtersen, a small village in the Hanover area. In 1937, he chose to join the cavalry. Fahnenjunker (cadet) Drewes soon found himself in Panzer-Regiment 6 and the following year he was a tank commander in this unit. As a young officer, Lt. Drewes then applied for the Luftwaffe and entered 4./ZG 76 "Haïfisch" (shark-mouthed Bf 110s) in 1940. The novice

The Bf 110C of Lt. Drewes undergoing maintenance at Jever, where 4./ZG 76 was stationed from September 1940 until its departure for Iraq in May 1941.

Bf 110D-3 fighters of Sonderkommando Junck in Mosul, May 1941.

Bf 110E "D5+IR" of 7./NJG 3 still carries the shark's mouth marking of 4./ZG 76. This variant of the Bf 110 was used by III. Gruppe until the autumn of 1943.

Oblt. Martin Drewes pictured in the spring of 1943 after his fourth victory. His first two successes were at the expense of RAF fighters while flying as a day fighter with 4./ZG 76.

participated mainly in maritime patrols over the North Sea. In May 1941, his *Staffel* was designated as part of the Sonderkommando Junck, a unit created from scratch to support Iraqi insurgents led by Rachid Ali Ghailani, fighting against the British. On May 20, 1941, Drewes claimed his first victory over an RAF Gloster Gladiator, although it is likely that the RAF machine was only damaged. Six days later, with no spares or support, the German fighters were unserviceable, and the expeditionary force was soon repatriated to Germany by Ju 52s. The second day victory notched up by Lt. Drewes was reportedly achieved over a Spitfire on August 29, 1941 as II./ZG 76 bounced 19 Squadron Spitfires out searching low over the sea for their CO, Sqn Ldr Lawson, who had been reported missing the previous day during a raid on Rotterdam.

In comparison to what awaited him in Germany, the Iraqi expedition appeared with hindsight to be nothing more than an "absurd and harmless" adventure. During 1942, in the night skies of Germany, RAF bombing raids were increasing in intensity. Wolfgang Falck had promoted the establishment of a night fighter arm and the German high command transferred most of the Falck's *Zerstörer* comrades into this new branch, ZG 76 being redesignated as NJG 3. One of their first actions was a daylight mission over the English Channel—in the three days February 11–13, 1942, Drewes took part in Operation *Donnerkeil*, the Channel "breakout" by the Kriegsmarine warships *Scharnhorst*, *Gneisenau*, and *Prinz Eugen*. The ships departed Brest and headed for Scandinavia through the Channel, the Luftwaffe successfully furnishing round-the-clock fighter cover.

By night Drewes proved to be an excellent tactician. The primary armament of the night fighters was the upward-firing cannon, the so-called "Schräge Musik" (lit. strange music). Pilots preferred it to the nose guns since it virtually guaranteed success, while there was a much smaller risk of being spotted and fired upon by the rear gunner. The approach from the side and below, whether guided by radar or from the ground, allowed the night fighters a better opportunity to spot the enemy against the lightness of the sky, and from there, descend under the bomber and match his speed before unleashing a salvo into the bomber's engines. In February 1943 he was appointed Staffelkapitän of 7./NJG 3.

In late 1943/early 1944, USAAF daytime attacks increased significantly. The Luftwaffe high command at this point decided to commit night fighters by day—in bad weather the day fighter force was often unable to take off as most fighter pilots were not trained on instruments. The night fighters were subsequently launched against powerful B-17 and B-24 formations. At the controls of his Bf 110 transformed into a *Tagzerstörer* (daytime heavy fighter), Drewes claimed seven American four-engine *Viermots* (three were not confirmed).

On May 5, 1944, *Kommodore* of NJG 1 Hans-Joachim Jabs assembled his *Gruppenkommandeure* at his Deelen HQ for a day of relaxation. Georg Greiner, lying down, plays the clown in front of his comrades. Standing from left: Erich Weissflog and Heinz Schnaufer (IV. Gruppe), Martin Drewes (III. Gruppe), Major Sutor (logistics officer), "Achim" Jabs (*Geschwaderkommodore*), Wilhelm Dormann (*Geschwaderstab*), Paul Forster (I. Gruppe), Eckard von Bonin (II. Gruppe), and Walter Knickmeier (operations officer). (Collection Fengler family)

On the morning of July 26, 1943, we were ordered to get airborne to intercept an inbound enemy bomber formation. Their objective was reported as most probably the city of Hamburg. I took off from Stade at 11:20 a.m. Our force of around 15 machines was led by the *Gruppenkommandeur* III./NJG 3, Hauptmann Milius. I was flying "tail-end Charlie," bringing up the rear of our formation. We came upon the bomber formation in the vicinity of Cuxhaven, and I was fully expecting the *Kommandeur* to prepare to engage the bombers—nothing of the sort happened. Over the radio I announced, "Jettisoning auxiliary fuel tank" and dove steeply away in pursuit of a *Pulk* of B-17s heading homewards. Their formation had opened up considerably. This was not of course anything like hunting an individual bomber, but still a question of attacking an entire formation that had simply spread out as they had come under flak fire. I was heading approximately towards Bremen. As I came back into land at Stade at 13:20 I could see that the remainder of our formation was already on the ground. I had only one question: "Why was no attack flown?" The response wasn't quite what I was expecting. Summoned by the *Kommandeur* and his adjutant, I was accused of having endangered our force by my cowardly actions in turning and running. My cowardice would not go unpunished. I was barred from the Officers' Kasino [mess] with immediate effect. I spoke up at this point. I replied that in that case it was my intention to institute court martial proceedings against myself. Initially the matter appeared to go no further. However, about two weeks later, around midday, I was summoned to the mess. To my observation that I was barred, I was told that an officer from another unit with the rank of *Hauptmann* was requesting to speak to me there. Entering the Kasino, I came upon a beaming Hauptmann Sigmund. He immediately grasped my hands, shook them vigorously and offered me his congratulations. He told me that Hptm. Jabs had been appointed *Kommandeur* IV./NJG 1 and that I was fly to Leeuwarden immediately to take over "his" 11. Staffel as *Staffelkapitän*. This was indeed

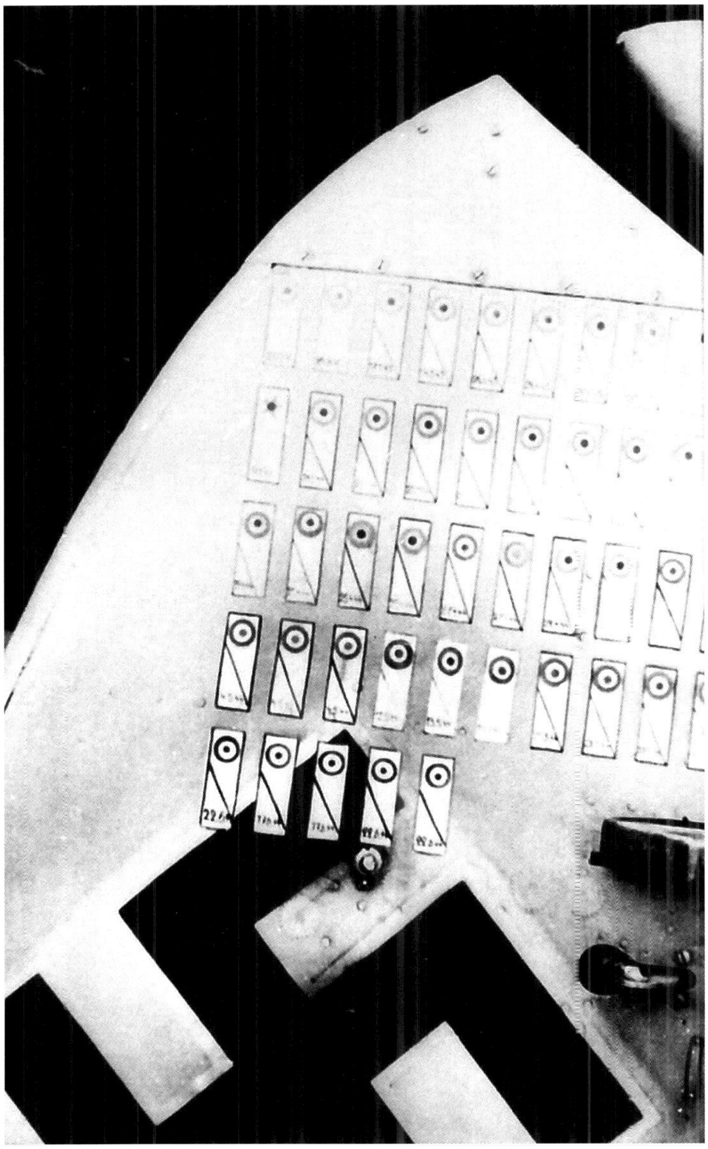

This vertical stabilizer with 45 victories is that of the Bf 110G-4 "G9+WD" flown by Drewes. The last four victories were on June 17 and 22, 1944, indicating that one of his claims has yet to be certified.

Two views of Hptm. Martin Drewes in late July 1944 at Leeuwarden next to his Bf 110G-4 "G9+WD" with 47 victory bars on its tail; on the right, his radio operator Ofw. Georg Petz. By this date he had already achieved 48 victories and the Knight's Cross displayed on the rudder was officially awarded to him on July 27, 1944. The *Kommandeu*r of III./NJG 1 had two aircraft assigned to him. "G9+MD" was lost on the night of July 14. Drewes ended the war with 49 *Luftsiege*, 43 of which were at night.

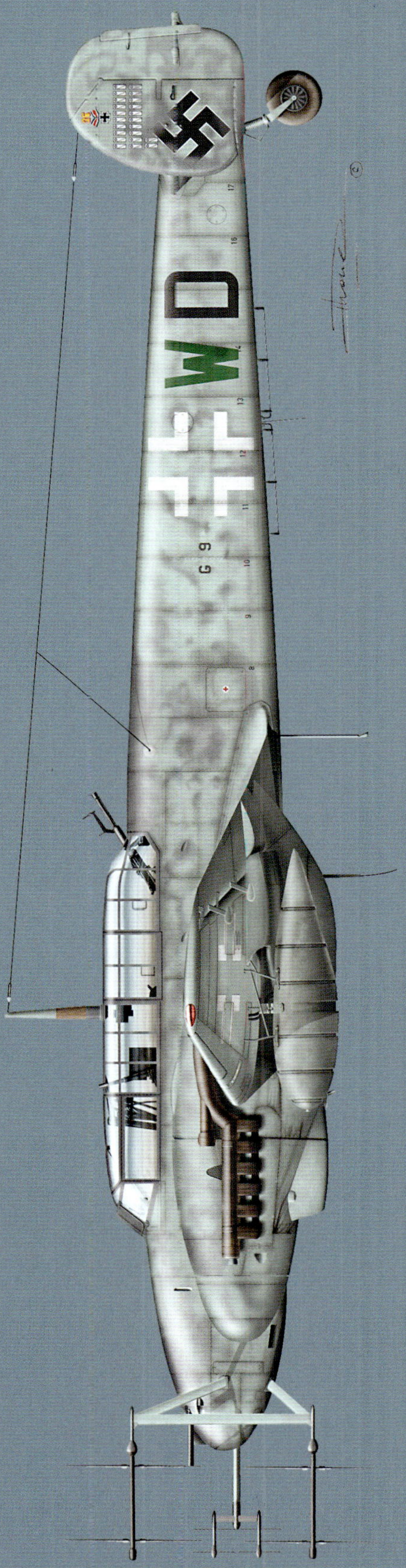

Hptm. Martin Drewes flew this Bf 110G-4 "G9+WD" as Kommandeur of III./NJG 1. Drewes survived the war and passed away in 2013.

> happy news. In addition, Hauptmann Sigmund explained that he had been appointed *Kommandeur* of III./NJG 3 with immediate effect and that Hptm. Milius had been transferred. As it turned out, my *Abschussmeldungen*—combat victory reports—for July 26, 1943, had not been forwarded but had gone missing (or been destroyed?). I wrote out both reports again and filed them. Hauptmann Sigmund was shot down during the night of October 3, 1943, so I never received any further news as to the progress of these two claims submissions. Neither did I attempt to follow the matter up. It was enough for me to know that these two bombers would never again drop their deadly cargoes on German cities—as it was, both victory reports bore my own signature and accurately reflected the facts as they occurred. With the move to IV./NJG 1, the night-fighting period began in earnest for me: my responsibilities grew ever bigger, while the general situation grew ever more difficult.

Appointed *Kommandeur* of III./NJG 1 on March 3, 1944, Drewe recorded an impressive series of successes against RAF Bomber Command throughout the spring and summer of 1944.

On the night of July 20/21, 1944, after claiming two further victories (his 47th and 48th), he detected an unsuspecting Lancaster in the bomber stream and flew a conventional *Schräge Musik* attack from below. Just as he opened fire, the bomber initiated a right turn, and the two- to three-second salvo slammed into the bomb bay—still loaded with its deadly cargo. The bomber disintegrated, and took Drewes and his crew with it, his Bf-110G-4 "G9+MD" heavily damaged and ablaze. Along with his crew—radio operator Obfw. Georg "Schorsch" Petz, and machine-gunner, Fw. Erich Handke—Drewes parachuted clear over Haarle. His left arm was broken, and his night vision would never be the same again. One piece of shrapnel had struck the wristwatch worn by gunner Petz, stopping it right at the moment of the explosion: 0119 hours.

A week later Drewes was awarded the Knight's Cross (July 27, 1944) for his 48 victories; the Oak Leaves followed on April 17, 1945, for 49 *Luftsiege* obtained in 235 combat sorties. After the war, unable to find work in the ruins of post-war Germany, he went into self-imposed exile in Brazil, where he resumed his activity as a civilian pilot until his retirement. Drewes passed away on October 13, 2013.

Drewes' victories

No	Date	Time	Aircraft	Unit	Place
1	May 20, 1941		Gladiator		Fallujah area (Iraq)
2	Aug 29, 1941	1100	Spitfire	19 Sqn	North Sea
3	Jan 17, 1943	2232	Lancaster I 55630	83 Sqn	nr Linten
4	Mar 14, 1943	2142	Halifax II DT620	138 Sqn	Storre Heddinge
5	Jun 26, 1943	0240	Lancaster II ED943	57 Sqn	Den Hoorn/Texel
6	Aug 27, 1943	0110	Halifax II JD731	77 Sqn	Auvelais
7	Aug 31, 1943	0358	Halifax V DK207	76 Sqn	Grathem
8	Sep 27, 1943	2330	Halifax V LK919	434 Sqn	Stadthagen
9	Nov 26, 1943	1247	B-17	423rd BS/306th BG	nr Lemmer
10	Jan 5, 1944	1232	B-24	714th or 715th BS/448th BG	off Nordeney
11	Jan 11, 1944	0041	B-17	339th BS/96th BG	off The Hague
12		0320	B-17	369th BS/306th BG	Almelo
13	Jan 14, 1944	1838	Lancaster III DV287	101 Sqn	Klazienaveen

14	Jan 22, 1944	0046	Lancaster II DS824	514 Sqn	Ijselmeer
15	Mar 24, 1944	2358	Lancaster III ND671	57 Sqn	Lippstadt
16	Mar 25, 1944	0020	Lancaster III ND641	625 Sqn	Twente
17		0037	Lancaster II LL694	115 Sqn	Deventer
18	Mar 31, 1944	0005	Lancaster III LM376 467 or LM425	550 Sqn	Spa
19		0050	Lancaster III W5006	9 Sqn	Megelburg
20		0120	Lancaster III ND390	97 Sqn	Coburg
21	Apr 19, 1944	0001	Halifax III LV956	466 Sqn	NE of Rouen
22		0011	Halifax III LW722	640 Sqn	SE of Dieppe
23	Apr 21, 1944	0040	Lancaster III ND564	207 Sqn	SE of Paris
24	Apr 23 1944	0027	Lancaster III JA933	582 Sqn	nr Compiègne
25	Apr 25, 1944	0037	Lancaster I ME693	622 Sqn	nr Kaiserslautern
26	Apr 27, 1944	0035	Lancaster III ND850	106 Sqn	Langres
27		0050	Lancaster		Biberach
28	Apr 28, 1944	0148	Lancaster (?)		nr Aachen
29	May 2, 1944	0045	Lancaster I ME689	75 Sqn	Saint-Arnoult
30	May 4, 1944	0026	Lancaster III ND360 or JA901	460 or 467 Sqn	NE of Troyes
31		0036	Lancaster III LM480	50 Sqn	St-Mesmin
32		0044	Lancaster I ME728	460 Sqn	Avant-lès-Marcilly
33		0050	Lancaster		nr Romilly
34		0118	Lancaster III EE185	44 Sqn	S of Troyes
35	May 13, 1944	0044	Lancaster X KB710	419 Sqn	Rhode-St-Genèse
36		0049	Halifax III MZ629	431 Sqn	Halle
37		0109	Halifax III LW682	426 Sqn	Schendelbeke
38	May 22, 1944	0050	Lancaster I ME722	103 Sqn	Hasselt-Zwolle
39		0058	Lancaster III JB672	630 Sqn	nr Deventer
40		0138	Lancaster II LL695	514 Sqn	Veghel
41		0150	Lancaster III ND559	156 Sqn	off The Hague
42		0204	Lancaster III ND579	166 Sqn	80km SW Ijmuiden
43	Jun 17, 1944	0246	Halifax III NA545	77 Sqn	off Ijmuiden
44		0247	Halifax III NA508	77 Sqn	Amstelveen
45	Jun 22, 1944	0232	Lancaster III ND683	49 Sqn	nr Schouwen
46		0236	Lancaster III LM578	207 Sqn	
47	Jul 21, 1944	0111	Halifax III MZ511	578 Sqn	Apeldoorn
48		0120	Lancaster III PB174	405 Sqn	Tubbergen
49	Mar 3, 1945	2213	Lancaster I	207, 227 or 463 Sqn	W of Münster

Oblt. Egmont zur Lippe-Weissenfeld after the award of the Knight's Cross on April 16, 1942, for his 21 victories. He was then *Staffelkapitän* of 5./NJG 2. (Collection Wim Govaerts)

Major Egmont zur Lippe-Weissenfeld

Egmont zur Lippe-Weissenfeld, born on July 14, 1918, in Salzburg, was a member of the Austrian Catholic nobility. His father, Alfred Rudolf, was Prince of Lippe-Weissenfeld with the rank of Serene Highness, while his mother was Countess Anna Goëss, a famous name in the Austro-Hungarian Empire. Egmont, the only son of four children, spent his youth in the mountains and forests of the Austrian Alps, learning at an early age to hunt like any good nobleman. He was also a music lover and a great sportsman, assiduously practicing gymnastics, skiing, sailing and later gliding after joining the Salzburg aeroclub in 1936. After passing his school leaving exam, he joined the Austrian Army the same year. Initially an infantryman, the prince joined the Graz flying school and then the Wiener-Neustadt flying school. After the Anschluss, the small Austrian Air Force was, unsurprisingly, incorporated in the Luftwaffe. His training continued at the

Bf 110D-0 "G9+CM" of 4./NJG 1. Egmont obtained his first two victories with this machine: a Wellington of No. 155 Squadron shot down on November 17, 1940, and a Whitley of No. 58 Squadron, on January 15, 1941.

Luftkriegschule in Fürstenfeldbruck. On September 1, 1939, at the time of the invasion of Poland, he was promoted to *Leutnant*. At the end of 1939, he trained in air combat in Schleissheim, Bavaria, before attending blind-flying courses at Vienna-Aspern.

On August 4, 1940, Lt. Lippe-Weissenfeld was posted to a *Zerstörer* unit, II./ZG 76, based in Düsseldorf. However, he quickly transferred to Nachtjagdgeschwader 1, undoubtedly the most famous Luftwaffe night fighter unit of World War II. "Egi" flew in 3. and then in 4./NJG 1 at Gütersloh with the rank of *Oberleutnant*. In October, he was entrusted with the direction of a *Sonderkommando* (experimental unit) at Schiphol, Amsterdam airport. During the night of November 16/17,

Six stars of 5./NJG 2 in spring 1942. From left: Georg Greiner (51 victories), Leopold "Poldi" Fellerer (41 victories), Prinz zur Lippe-Weissenfeld (49 victories), Paul Gildner (44 victories), Oskar Köstler (6 victories) and Karl-Heinz Völlkopf (6 victories). Only Greiner and Fellerer would see the end of the war. (Collection G. Greiner)

Weissenfeld with the rudder of his Bf 110F W.Nr. 4620 showing a score of 33 victories. The last three victories were achieved on the night of July 2/3, 1942. The prince was adept at close-range attacks and *Von hinten unten* (from below and behind) tactics.

the young officer returned his first victory (a Wellington of No. 115 Squadron) with his faithful *Bordfunker*, radio operator Unteroffizier Josef Rennette. The two crew repeated the feat on the evening of January 15, 1941, opening fire at close range on a Whitley that crashed into flames in the large Callantsoog nature reserve. A few days later, Egmont met his future fiancée, Hannelore Ide, secretary at the Luftgaukommando Holland and a classical music lover like himself.

Combat was continuous during the spring of 1941. On April 10, shortly after midnight, Lippe-Weissenfeld was credited with a Wellington of No. 12 Squadron, the NJG's 1,100th *Luftsiege*. On May 11, he shot down a Stirling, his fifth night victory. By July 25 he had already doubled this figure. On June 30, the prince's Bf 110C-4 W.Nr. 2075 collided in mid-air with the 110 piloted by Lt. Schoenert during a training session. The Austrian ace and his *Bordfunker* escaped unscathed after jumping clear, taking an early bath in the Zuiderzee.

On November 1, 1941, Lippe-Weissenfeld took over 5. Staffel of NJG 2. During the night of November 7/8, he achieved his first double to the west of Alkmaar. On March 26/27, 1942, he was able to shoot down four British bombers. On April 16, he received the Knight's Cross for his 21 victories.

On October 1, he was promoted to *Kapitän* of 11./NJG 1, while a Lancaster of No. 467 Squadron, shot down northwest of Heligoland on May 14, 1943, constituted his 40th air victory. On June 1, he became *Kommandeur* of III./NJG 1, which was based at Twente. On the 13th of the same month, he shot down two Halifax bombers over Germany and on August 2, the "Prince of the Night" was summoned to Hitler's headquarters to receive the Oak Leaves. He had obtained his 45th victory three days earlier. On December 16, he added two Berlin-bound Lancasters to his score.

Briefing at the NJG 5 HQ in Parchim. The *Kommodore* shows clear resignation on his face. In a letter to his fiancée Hannelore on Christmas Eve, he wrote: "Last night we lost another good comrade. But I guess that's part of the deal ..." On March 12, 1944, the aviator prince lost control of his Bf 110G-4, which crashed near Saint-Hubert, in the Belgian Ardennes. He had 49 victories to his credit. (P. K. Helmut Grosse)

At the beginning of 1944, "Egi" enjoyed a month's rest. On February 20, he was promoted to the rank of *Major* and appointed *Kommodore* of NJG 5, a *Geschwader* based in Parchim. On March 12, 1944, he decided to visit his former comrades of III./NJG 1 at Laon-Athies. He took off at the controls of his Bf 110G-4 W.Nr. 720010 "C9+CD." Over the Ardennes, the Messerschmitt ran into a thick fog before being caught in a snowstorm. Egmont lost control of the aircraft which came down near Saint-Hubert. The prince, Oberfeldwebel Josef Rennette, and Unteroffizier Kurt Röber perished in the accident. The bodies were recovered by a German unit and buried in the Netherlands. They currently rest in Ijsselsteyn. Two of the *Major*'s sisters have always contested the official version, based on witnesses who saw an explosion in the sky. For them, there was much more behind his death. Was the hero of the Nachtjagd sabotaged for belonging to the old nobility that Hitler despised so much? This seems unlikely. Egmont zur Lippe-Weissenfeld simply met a tragic end like many airmen during the conflict. Undefeated in combat, he had shot down 52 British bombers, 49 of which were officially credited.

Lippe-Weissenfeld's victories

No	Date	Time	Aircraft	Unit	Place
1	Nov 17, 1940	0205	Wellington IC P9286	115 Sqn	10km W of Medemblik
2	Jan 15, 1941	2246	Whitley V N1521	58 Sqn	5km N of Petten
3	Apr 10, 1941	0059	Wellington II W5375	12 Sqn	S of Den Helder
4	May 9, 1941	0248	Wellington IC R1226	: 214 Sqn	Anna Paulowna
5	May 11, 1941	0020	Stirling I N3654	15 Sqn	10km SW of Medemblik
6	Jun 13, 1941	0110	Whitley V T4279	77 Sqn	2km N of Medemblik
7	Jun 19, 1941	0053	Wellington IC R1696	305 Sqn	W of Enkhuizen
8	Jun 23, 1941	0213	Wellington IC T2990	311 Sqn	Insinghuizen
9	Jul 14, 1941	0028	Wellington IC R1502	115 Sqn	S of Medemblik
10	Jul 25, 1941	0223	Wellington IC X9620	304 Sqn	3km SW of Medemblik
11	Jul 26, 1941	0320	Whitley V Z6624	10 Sqn	11km De Kooi
12	Nov 8, 1941	2303	Whitley V Z6567	51 Sqn	18km W Alkmaar
13		0041	Wellington IC R1606	150 Sqn	E Medemblik
14		0120	Wellington IV Z1211	142 Sqn	W Alkmaar
15	Dec 27, 1941	2146	Whitley V Z6841	58 Sqn	at sea off Petten
16	Feb 24, 1942	2149	Hampden I AT194	144 Sqn	N of Terschelling
17		2202	Hampden X2969	144 Sqn	
18	Mar 26, 1942	2227	Wellington IV Z1269	300 Sqn	De Koog
19		2240	Wellington II W5372	12 Sqn	SW of Grotebroek
20		2255	Wellington IV R1590	301 Sqn	N of Ijmuiden
21		2316	Wellington		Edam area

22	Jun 4, 1942	0050	Wellington III X3724	115 Sqn	SW Vieland
23	Jun 7, 1942	0147	Stirling I N3761	214 Sqn	Terschelling
24	Jun 12, 1942	0308	Lancaster I R5636	83 Sqn	N Ameland
25	Jun 21, 1942	0143	Halifax II W1114	76 Sqn	25km NW Groningen
26		0145	Wellington III X3713	9 Sqn	2km NW Groninge
27		0156	Wellington III X3760	75 Sqn	N Ameland
28	Jun 26, 1942	0105	Wellington IC T2723	20 OTU	Terschelling
29		0152	Hudson V AM794	1 OTU	10km N Vlieland
30	Jun 30, 1942	0308	Wellington III X3539	75 Sqn	S Ameland
31	Jul 3, 1942	0054	Hampden I AT248	420 Sqn	S Koudum
32		0109	Wellington IV Z1470	460 Sqn	N Urk
33		0220	Wellington IC AD605	109 Sqn	Dirkshorn
34	Jul 20, 1942	0252	Halifax II W1162	158 Sqn	N Terschelling
35	Aug 28, 1942	0150	Wellington III X3657	101 Sqn	over the sea
36	Sep 5, 1942	0339	Halifax II W1220	103 Sqn	5km SW Leeuwarden
37	Sep 23, 1942	2336	Wellington IV Z1219	142 Sqn	NW Vlieland
38	Jan 17, 1943	2213	Lancaster I R5843	1654 HCU	5km N Leer
39	Jan 22, 1943	2213	Halifax II DT621 or DT583	76 or 158 Sqn	NNW Emden or off Borkum
40	May 14 1943	0111	Lancaster III ED543	467 Sqn	12km NNW of Helgoland
41	Jun 13, 1943	0122	Halifax II JB790	408 Sqn	3km NW of Burgsteinfurt
42		0134	Halifax V DK177	76 Sqn	6km N Nienburg
43	Jun 23, 1943	0247	Stirling I EF399	75 Sqn	N Ameland
-		0255	Stirling		10km N Vlieland
44	Jul 30, 1943	0140	Lancaster III ED535	460 Sqn	Hägbluer Holz
-	Aug 3, 1943	0226	Halifax		20km S of Stade
45	Sep 6, 1943	0030	Stirling III EE893	75 Sqn	7km SE Hassloch
	Sep 23, 1943	2336	Wellington		7km S Hengelo
46	Sep 29 1943	2144	Halifax V DK259	434 Sqn	NW Borkelo
47		2155	Halifax V LK634	434 Sqn	2km NW Leiden
48	Dec 16, 1943	1850	Lancaster III LM424	625 Sqn	N Ahlhorn
49		1900	Lancaster III JB543	7 Sqn	NW Nordhorn

Hauptmann Ludwig Meister

Ludwig "Luk" Meister, the second son of an industrialist, was born on December 14, 1919, in Erbendorf, Bavaria. After completing his schooling in Regensburg, he hoped to join the Luftwaffe to satisfy his desire to fly, and to this end he took various exams in 1937. However, he was not accepted until late, on October 1, 1939, one month after the start of World War II. After his *Rekrutenzeit* (basic training), Meister went to various schools: Weimar-Nohra, Dresden-Klotsche, Altenburg, Brandis, Kamenz, and Neubiberg. It was in the latter *Zerstörer Flugschule* that he was to team up with his radio gunner, Fw. Hannes Forke from Leipzig. As a crew the pair flew together until the end of the war. In mid-July 1941, Meister was posted to Stuttgart-Echterdingen, headquarters of the Ergänzungsstaffel/NJG 1, the NJG 1 training unit. The two crewmembers were thus steered towards the Nachtjagd, the night fighter arm. In September, the two newcomers were transferred to 5./NJG 1 based in St. Trond. Meister soon claimed three victories over northern Germany, two of which were officially confirmed. In February 1942, the Bavarian and his comrade were part of the escorting force accompanying the "breakout" of the German battleships from the French Atlantic port of Brest. Sailing through the Straits of Dover during bad weather, the Kriegsmarine vessels forced their way through the English Channel to Scandinavia (Operation *Donnerkeil*). In May 1942, Meister and his radio operator were transferred to III./NJG 4 based in Mainz-Finthen. Three more victories were then achieved, again over Germany. On October 2, 1942, the Meister–Forcke crew

Ludwig Meister with his faithful radio operator, Hannes Forke. The latter is wearing glasses, rare among Luftwaffe flying personnel.

The Meister–Forke crew initially flew with 5./NJG 1 on the Bf 110 "G9+IN."

departed for France. The two young men were transferred to the Stab I./NJG 4 operating out of Laon-Athies. Meister had become friends with his *Kommandeur*, Major Wilhelm Herget. The Bf 110s based in Laon were the outposts of the night defense of the Reich, protecting Germany from RAF bombers and operating almost every night over northern France and Belgium. Eleven victories would follow. In 1942, to fill a gap in the Reich's night defenses, an airfield was built in southern Belgium, at Florennes. As soon as this *Fliegerhorst* (airbase) was operational in early 1943, I./NJG 4 was established there. As a result of his combat successes, Oblt. Meister took command of 1. Staffel. As the RAF intensified its actions in 1943 with the aim of destroying German cities and industry, Meister's record of achievement grew. In early 1944, Berlin became the priority target of RAF Bomber Command and I./NJG 4 spent some time away from Belgium, at Werneuchen, to reinforce the defense of the capital of the Reich. "Luk" Meister returned with his unit to Florennes in February 1944 and went back into action. On March 23, 1944, however, returning by day to Florennes from northern Germany where he had been pursuing Allied bombers, he was shot down over Naninne (near Namur) by a USAAF P-47. Seriously wounded, he underwent a long convalescence. On June 9, 1944, he was awarded the Knight's Cross for his 37 nighttime successes. On December 6, 1944, Hptm. Meister returned to action and was promoted to *Kommandeur* of III/NJG 4, winning his last victory in March 1945 near Kassel. On May 4, he was awarded one last distinction before the cessation of hostilities: the Fighter Pilot's Clasp in Gold. III./NJG 4 was based in the north of Germany. Meister lost most of his documents and photos, as his possessions were stored in a barn that was looted by prisoners of war who had been released from a nearby camp. This explains why there are so few photos of this aviator.

The two young aviators proudly photographed their aircraft with the application of their first victory bar obtained on the night of November 30, 1941.

Messerschmitt Bf 110D "G9+IN" of Lt. Ludwig Meister, 5./NJG 1, St. Trond, early December 1941.

A second victory on the same night was later confirmed, allowing them to add a second bar to the vertical stabilizer of their Bf 110. Forke poses in front of their new aircraft, which still bears its *Stammkennzeichen* or factory codes.

First two *Abschussbalken* close up. These are the only personal photos of a rudder marking for this crew after the airmen lost all their their personal documents.

Meister on his Bf 110 displaying the Nachtjagd badge.

As III./NJG 4 was still operational on May 8, 1945, the *Gruppe* was considered by the Allied authorities to have surrendered "in the field" and its members were soon released. Unemployed, Meister was lucky enough to find work in the Stuttgart publishing house owned by his unfailing friend Herget as a senior manager, remaining there until his retirement. When he retired, he built a villa in the Var in the South of France. He spent many pleasant years in the sun before returning to his native Bavaria where he died on November 26, 2011.

His former crewmember Hannes Forke, who was largely involved in Meister's success as a radio and then radar operator and gunner, drowned in the 1960s on a beach in the Netherlands while attempting to rescue his daughter and nephew who had been swept away by the current.

Meister's record of achievements included 39 confirmed victories, comprising five twin-engine machines, 33 RAF four-engine bombers, and one Boeing B-17 shot down by day.

"Luk" Meister with the Knight's Cross received on June 9, 1944.

Meister's victories

No	Date	Time	Aircraft	Unit	Place
1	Nov 30, 1941	2244	Halifax I L9582	35 Sqn	Lentföhrden
2		2314	Whitley V Z6575	58 Sqn	30km NW of Stade
-		2325	Wellington		Hamburg
3	Aug, 29, 1942	0015	Wellington B III	115 Sqn	Eich
4		0043	Stirling I N6081	149 Sqn	Airlenbach
5			Wellington		Simmern
6	Oct 25, 1942	0254	Wellington III BJ725	75 Sqn	Bavay
7	Nov 22, 1942	2046	Lancaster I W4360	57 Sqn	Tourinnes-Saint-Lambert

8	Dec 3/4, 1942		Halifax		Couvron-et-Aumencourt
9	Dec 21/22, 1942		Stirling	7 Sqn	Channel
10	Mar 9, 1943	0030	Halifax II W7851	35 Sqn	nr Cateau-Cambrésis
11	Apr 17, 1943	0408	Halifax II DT752	408 (RCAF) Sqn	Nassogne
12	May 30, 1943	0207	Stirling I EF 349	90 Sqn	Proville
13	Jun 26, 1943	0145	Stirling II BK767	214 Sqn	3km SE of Alten
14	Jul 4, 1943	0240	Halifax II JD262	51 Sqn	Rance
15	Jul 14, 1943	0230	Halifax II JD297	102 Sqn	Wattignies-la-Victoire
16	Aug 28, 1943	0135	Lancaster III ED627	207 Sqn	Wolperthausen
17		0157	Lancaster		Nuremberg
18	Oct 4, 1943	2102	Halifax V LK931	428 Sqn	Obereisenbach
19		2105	Halifax		nr Trier
20			Halifax		nr 21km W of Cologne Cologne
21	Nov 3, 1943	1957	Halifax V EB257	434 Sqn	
22	Nov 23, 1943	2016	Lancaster III JB528	103 Sqn	Grebs
23	Jan 2, 1944	0515	Lancaster III ND384	156 Sqn	Estinnes-au-Val
24		0536	Lancaster III JA925	156 Sqn	4km off Saint-Pol-sur-Mer
25		0551	Lancaster I JB737	405 Sqn	Croix
26		0600	Lancaster I W4897	463 Sqn	off Saint-Pol-sur-Mer
27	Jan 7, 1944	1300	B-17	8th USAF	nr Cambrai
28	Jan 20, 1944	1920	Lancaster		Schönmark
29		1937	Halifax		SW Liebenwalde
30	Feb 20, 1944	0248	Halifax III HX325 or LW501	35 or 158 Sqn	13km Wesendorf NE of Celle
31		0319	Halifax		
32	Feb 21, 1944	0317	Lancaster III ND338	630 Sqn	Plittersdorf
33	Feb 25, 1944	2055	Lancaster III ND250	44 Sqn	Béthancourt
34		2059	Lancaster I DV294	61 Sqn	SW of Menil-Annelles
35		2114	Lancaster III DV274	463 Sqn	SSW of Vouziers
36	Mar 16, 1944	0118	Lancaster III ND681	100 Sqn	Bonneuil-les-Eaux
37		0130	Lancaster III ND583	630 Sqn	S of Besmé
38	Mar 23, 1944	2151	Lancaster		nr Saint-Omer
39	Mar 7, 1945	2030	Lancaster		nr Kassel

Afterword

The widespread practice of marking up aerial victories on combat aircraft—during both World War I and, even more so, World War II—did not disappear after 1945.

However, it would never again be seen on the scale of those two conflicts. Fortunately, post-1945 wars remained retrospectively limited in time or territory. Nevertheless, whether in Korea, Vietnam, the Middle East, or the Falklands, aircraft from several nations fought each other and, proud of their successes, the victors of these engagements had their aircraft (now jets) painted with victory markings which, although often quite different from those of their predecessors, maintained this tradition of combat aviation. "Old soldiers never die …"

Bibliography

Bergström, C. *Black Cross Red Star: Air War Over the Eastern Front*. Classic Publications 2008.

Bergström, C. *Bagration to Berlin: The Final Air Battles in the East, 1944–45*. Classic Publications 2008.

Boiten, Theo. *Nachtjagd War Diaries* (2 vols.). Red Kite 2008.

Caldwell, Donald. *Day Fighters in Defence of the Reich: A War Diary, 1942–45*. Frontline Books 2011.

Manrho, John & Pütz, Ron. *Bodenplatte: The Luftwaffe's Last Hope*. Hikoki 2004.

Mathews, Andrew & Foreman, John. *Luftwaffe Aces* (4 vols.). Red Kite 2014.

Obermaier, Ernst. *Die Ritterkreuzträger der Luftwaffe 1939–1945*. Dieter Hoffmann 1966.

Page, Neil. *Day Fighter Aces of the Luftwaffe* (2 vols.). Casemate Illustrated 2020.

Ries, Karl & Obermaier, Ernst. *Bilanz am Seitenleitwerk*. Dieter Hoffmann 1970.

Roba, Jean-Louis. *The Luftwaffe in Africa*. Casemate Illustrated 2019.

Saintes, Philippe. *La Jagdgeschwader 54, l'escadre au cœur vert* (2 vols.). Lela Presse 2017.

Scutts, Jerry. *Jagdgeschwader 54: Aces of the Eastern Front*. Airlife Publishing 1992.

Shores, Christopher. *Air Aces*. Bison Books 1983.

Williams, David. *Hunters of the Reich: Day Fighters*. Cerberus 2002.

The only USAF ace of the Vietnam war, Captain Richard "Steve" Ritchie, poses in front of his F-4 Phantom after his fifth victory. Note the five large red stars marking his successes in combat. (Jean-Louis Roba)

Index